Contents

About this book

This examination practice book has been written to help you prepare for the Stage III RSA Text Processing Modular Award in Document Presentation. The book is divided into two sections.

■ 1 Preparing for examinations

This section provides you with details of the equipment required for the document presentation examination as well as hints and tips on advance preparation and how best to approach the examination. It also provides you with a list of errors which will incur faults in the examination and the opportunity to practise your proof reading skills which should be applied to any work you produce.

The Stage III Document Presentation examination requires you to recall previously saved files and make amendments as instructed. The files you will need for the document presentation mock examination papers in this book are shown in this section and can be used to practise your keyboarding and accuracy skills.

■ 2 Document Presentation

This section provides details of the Document Presentation Part 2 examination at Stage III and seven mock examination papers to help you prepare for the examination.

Format of the book

Some of the tasks in this book may be more demanding than those you will meet in the examination. This will help you to develop your confidence and ability to succeed in the examination.

Worked examples for all the exercises are provided at the back of the book (pages 97–126) so that you can check your own work. The printed worked examples in this book are reduced to A6 size and displayed two to a page.

DOCUMENT PRESENTATION EXAM PRACTICE

STAGE III

SHARON SPENCER

Heinemann Educational Publishers
Halley Court, Jordan Hill, Oxford OX2 8EJ
A division of Reed Educational & Professional Publishing Ltd

Heinemann is a registered trademark of Reed Educational & Professional Publishing
Limited

OXFORD MELBOURNE AUCKLAND JOHANNESBURG BLANTYRE GABORONE
IBADAN PORTSMOUTH NH (USA) CHICAGO

First published 1999
2003 2002 2001 2000 99
10 9 8 7 6 5 4 3 2 1

A catalogue record for this book is available from the British Library on request.

ISBN 0 435 45396 3

Designed by Jackie Hill
Typeset by TechType, Abingdon, Oxon
Printed and Bound in Great Britain by Thomson Litho Ltd, East Kilbride, Scotland

0769166   651.85

Author Acknowledgements

I would like to thank all those who helped in the preparation of this book, particularly
Rosalyn Bass at Heinemann Educational for her advice and encouragement. I would
also like to thank my family – Ian, Lucy and Joseph for their help, support and
patience while writing this book.

Sharon Spencer

Preparing for examinations

Examinations can be stressful, no matter how well prepared you are. Remembering all the equipment and stationery you will need for the examination will help you remain calm on the day. Make a list of equipment required and check this off as you get your things ready.

Check with your centre which of the following it will provide.

- Dictionary.
- Computer manual – this may be a software manual or a centre-prepared set of notes. However, it must not contain any notes on theory.
- Ruler – showing both inches and millimetres/centimetres.
- Highlighter pen – this is useful for highlighting instructions and amendments to be made.
- Pen – for completing your answer book.
- Pencil – for writing notes on the examination paper.
- Correction pen, fluid or papers.

Advance preparation

You should try to eat something before the examination. Although you may not feel like eating beforehand, it will give you the energy to keep going. If you are hungry you may find you become tired half-way through.

You should, of course, be on time for your examination. Try to arrive at least 15 minutes before the start time so that you can get organised. There is nothing worse than arriving late and then having to get ready quickly – this will make you feel nervous.

Make sure you understand the centre's instructions for saving your files and printing, etc. Ask questions before the examination starts, to clarify these points if necessary.

If it is at all possible, have a five-minute 'warm-up'. Type some paragraphs of text to get your fingers moving quickly. This will also help you calm down. Do not worry if you make lots of mistakes at this point.

During the examination

Try to have your strategy planned before the examination begins. It is helpful if you start with a short and comparatively easy task. It is not usually a good idea to start with a task containing a table or complicated diagram. It can take a few minutes to get into the examination and so a simple task will build your confidence and help you relax. Use the time schedules given in this book to see how long you should spend on each task.

You should allow around five minutes of examination time to read the instructions carefully. It is often helpful to highlight the instructions with a highlighter pen before you start a task. This will act as a checklist and you will be able to tick off the instructions as you carry them out. Make a pencil note on the examination paper to remind you to insert page numbers, etc. Do not forget to check the examination paper carefully – there are often instructions dotted around the page.

If you do make a mistake try not to start the task again unless absolutely necessary. Do not forget that errors such as not leaving a space between words or forgetting to indicate a new paragraph will incur only one fault. If you start the task again and then fail to complete it, you will incur many more faults.

Remember that if you attempt each task you stand a chance of passing the examination – however, if there is a task missing you will automatically fail. This means you must check that all tasks are clearly labelled and included in your answer book.

In your time plan allow at least ten minutes for checking your work carefully. This is probably the most important part of the examination. One approach is to key in all the tasks and when you have finished run each task through the spell check. This will pick up any typographical or basic spelling errors. Then, spend any time remaining checking each piece of work carefully in case you have left out a sentence or failed to carry out an instruction. Check that you have numbered any continuation pages.

If your centre allows you to print your work during the examination, then do take advantage of this if time allows. It is often much easier to proof read printed work than check from the screen. If you are limited to the amount of paper you can use, do not forget you can print on the back of your sheets of paper. Although this is not ideal, you will only incur one fault and it is much better than not handing in a task.

Do not forget to type your full name, centre number and task number on each sheet of paper. You should complete your answer book very carefully, paying particular attention to writing your name clearly. This is where the examining body will get the information that appears on your certificate, so make sure your name is spelt correctly and is easy to read.

Good luck!

Proof reading skills

One of the most common reasons for candidates failing examinations is their failure to proof read carefully enough. Once you have finished typing a piece of work, you must read it through very carefully, checking it word for word against the examination paper.

This section aims to help you improve your proof reading skills by showing you the types of error that are commonly made in examinations. Test yourself by finding the errors in the proof reading exercises and then check them against the key at the back of the book. This will help you develop good proof reading skills and will point out where candidates often go wrong in examinations.

■ Typographical and spelling errors

Typographical errors are common typing mistakes such as transposing letters within a word. For example, 'hte' instead of 'the'. They are different from spelling errors and do not relate to how well a person can spell. Other examples of typographical errors include:

- not having a capital letter at the beginning of a sentence (poor use of the shift key)
- not leaving a space between words (failing to hit the space bar hard enough)
- too many spaces between words or spaces within words (hitting the space bar too hard)
- additional characters within a word (pressing a key too hard or leaving your finger on a key for too long)
- omission of a character(s) within a word (pressing the key too lightly)
- capital letters within words (hitting the shift key by mistake)
- incorrect letters used (having your fingers on the wrong keys to start with)
- transposing letters (trying to type too quickly)
- numbers appearing within words (having your fingers in the wrong place).

If you notice many typographical errors in your work it may be helpful to revise the keyboard and improve your typing technique. You do not need to go back to the beginning, just practise some typing drills each time you start to type. You only need to spend a few minutes each day on drills and you will soon notice the difference. The work you produce should become much more accurate and your typing speeds will increase.

If you are typing too quickly and are making many mistakes, then slow down a little. In the long run your work will be completed much more quickly if you do not have to go back to correct mistakes.

■ Spelling errors

If you know that spelling is not one of your strengths then you must check your work extra carefully.

Once you have completed a piece of work, use the spell check facility if you have one. This will help you to pick up any typographical errors and any obvious spelling mistakes. If there are words that are questioned, then check carefully to ensure you choose the correct alternative. This is particularly important if your spell check uses an American dictionary. If you are unsure then use an English dictionary to double-check. You must also check that you have typed the correct word if there are two meanings – for example, 'their' and 'there'.

■ Layout errors

There are many different layout errors that can be made. They include the following:

- ■ Failure to number continuation sheets.
- ■ Left-hand or top margins of less than 13 mm ($\frac{1}{2}$ in) or a ragged left-hand margin.
- ■ No clear line space before and after separate items.
- ■ Failure to start or close up a paragraph as indicated in the draft.
- ■ Inconsistent spacing between paragraphs.
- ■ Inconsistent use of time, money, weight, spellings, punctuation, words and figures within a document.
- ■ Incorrect emphasis of words or sentences.
- ■ Use of line spacing not as instructed.
- ■ Incorrect use of stationery.
- ■ Headings, references, etc not as shown in the draft.
- ■ Incorrect centring.
- ■ Initial capitals used incorrectly – either added or omitted.
- ■ Insetting of text carried out incorrectly.
- ■ Incorrect adjustment of line length.
- ■ Failure to allocate correct amount of space as instructed in the draft.
- ■ Failure to insert or shade text boxes.
- ■ Failure to insert borders.
- ■ Failure to type accents, fractions, symbols correctly.
- ■ Failure to use subscript and superscript characters correctly.
- ■ Failure to insert graphics/diagrams as instructed.
- ■ Failure to insert headers/footers as instructed.
- ■ Failure to use the specified house style.
- ■ Failure to change type size and style as instructed.
- ■ Failure to present information in columns as instructed.
- ■ Failure to insert additional text as instructed.

These faults are less common than accuracy errors, but you will need to check your work carefully against the examination paper to ensure that you avoid making any of them. If you are able to print during the examination, then you should do so. It is much easier to proof read a 'hard copy' than to check work on the screen. If you are not able to print your work, then use the 'print preview' facility so that you can see how your work looks before it is printed.

Proof Reading Practice Exercise 1

In the following document there are ten errors. When you have found them type a correct copy and check your proof reading skills with the key and error sheet shown at the back of the book.

First Impressions

You have decided to build your own home. The plans have been drawn up and the specification put together Before you sit back and relax, consider the driveway to your front door.

Remember thaat the driveway is the frist area of your home so ensure it compliments the type of home you have build and the materials you have used. There is a wide vareity of materials available, for example, blocks, Bricks, tarmac, shingle and crazy paving.

Before you decide on a design, consider the following:

- the gradient of the land
- the aspcet
- the access and egress to the highway and line across the footpath
  the surface water and drainage
- the line of the drive
- the trafffic flow in the road

Proof Reading Practice Exercise 2

In the following document there are twelve errors. When you have found them type a correct copy and check your proof reading skills with the key and error sheet shown at the back of the book.

SUNBURN

The number of cases of skin canser in the UK has risin sharply in the passed few year.   It is essential that you take care ofyour skin when in the sun.

Remember that even it if appears to be cloudy or windy the suns rays can penetrate through and cause damage to your skin.

It is important to use a sunblock if you are out and about in the sun. For the first few few days use a cream that has total protection and then gradulaly reduce this.

If you have been swmiming you may need to apply another layer of cream when you leave the pool. During the midday hours you should wear a T-shirt and hat.

Do not forget to protection your eyes. Sunglasses should be worn at all times.

Proof Reading Practice Exercise 3

In the following document there are eleven errors. When you have found them type a correct copy and check your proof reading skills with the key and error sheet shown at the back of the book.

CAREERS ADVISORY SERVICE

Looking for a new carrer?

Come to the

CAREER AND EMPLOYMENT FAYRE

at The Pavilion

6 – 8 March

9 am – 8 pm

Over 100 exhibitors together with careers advisery expert's will be on hand to give advice in the following career areas.

<u>Hospitality and Cattering</u>

This covers employment in many different fields.Hotels, restaurants, tourism and travel. We can give advise on the qualifications required and courses available.

Administration

If you would like to no more about careers in administration we can help. We have a number of Modern Apprentiseships places avaialbe in this employment sector.

<u>Computing</u>

There are many employment opportunity's in this growth area. Find out how to enter this exciting new market.

▮ Recalled text

Three of the documents in the Stage III Document Presentation examination will be recalled from previously saved files for you to make amendments as instructed.

The files you will need for the document presentation mock examination papers in this book should be typed exactly as shown in the draft documents which follow.

Save all the files under the file name given but do not print a copy.

In the examination, these documents will be keyed in by your tutor in advance. However, when working through this book, use these documents to practise your keyboarding and accuracy skills.

Recalled Text Exam Practice 1 Document 1

Key in the following document exactly as shown except for line endings which must be allowed to occur naturally. Save as HOME1.

HAVE YOU EVER WISHED YOU COULD BUILD YOUR OWN HOME?

you can!

MANY PEOPLE BUILD THEIR DREAM HOMES EACH YEAR.

how do they do it?

Sponsored by Design and Build™ Magazine

Timber-framed houses
Finding a suitable building plot
How to budget for the build
How to calculate the quantity of materials required.

Recalled Text Exam Practice 1 Document 3

Key in the following document exactly as shown except for line endings which must be allowed to occur naturally. Use single-line spacing and a ragged right-hand margin. The line length should be 15cm. Save as HOME3.

Choosing a suitable site

Although building your own home is a realistic dream, finding the right site can be a frustrating and time-consuming process.

Measuring the Site

When you find a potential building site, walk round it checking the boundaries and measurements. Ensure they are the same as on the sale details, the deeds and any planning permission.

This will give you the total site area. Remember that the proposed dwelling must fit easily onto the site including access.

Site Problems

Check the site for possible problems. These may include ponds, trees, areas of concrete, ditches, etc. Assess whether you can deal with these easily or whether they will add thousands of pounds to your building budget. Wet areas or a spring can also cause problems on the site. However, in dry weather, these may not be obvious immediately. Indicators can be willows, rushes or alders, although you should not jump to conclusions.

Services

If the land already has the main services connected (these are sewerage, gas, water and electricity) check the position of the various manholes, stopcocks and pipes. If these need to be diverted to accommodate your building this could prove expensive.

If there are no existing services check the immediate vicinity to see where they are. Connection fees can be very costly. Bear in mind that you have no automatic right to cross land that does not belong to you in order to connect the services.

Access

Obviously you will need to have adequate access to the site. If you are planning to buy a site on a private road you will need to obtain access rights. This can take time and money. You will also need to be able to have good visibility at the point you drive would join the public highway.

If any of these problems do come to light

Recalled Text Exam Practice 1 Document 4

Key in the following document exactly as shown except for line endings which must be allowed to occur naturally. Use a three-column (table) layout for the land items. Use single-line spacing and a ragged right-hand margin. Save as HOME4.

Land for Sale

The following plots of land are all suitable for building residential accommodation.

COUNTY	PLOT DETAILS	REF NO
Berkshire		
	Grade II listed thatched cottage in need of complete renovation. £100,000	BK1
Cambridgeshire		
	Four plots each with a site area of ½ acre. Each has outline planning permission for a detached dwelling. £50,000 per plot	CM1
Cheshire		
	Single building plot with outline planning permission for 3-bedroomed property. £39,000	CH1
Cornwall		
	Plot measuring 100ft x 63ft with lapsed outline planning permission for a single detached dwelling. The plot is located in a village inland. £55,000	CW2
	Beautiful sea views from this plot measuring $530m^2$. Detailed planning permission for a 2-storey, 3-bedroomed dwelling. £64,000	CW3
Suffolk		
	Chapel suitable for conversion. Total site area ¼ acre with outline planning permission granted. £85,000	SK1
Yorkshire		
	Site for sale totalling 1 acre. Outline planning permission granted for 3 detached, 2-storey dwellings. Owner will split into separate plots. £120,000 or £45,000 per plot.	YK1

Recalled Text Exam Practice 2 Document 1

Key in the following document exactly as shown except for line endings which must be allowed to occur naturally. Save as FOOD1.

Would you like to work with lots of people?

Do you enjoy a challenge?

Have you considered a career in catering?

If so, why not join one of our catering and hospitality courses?

Food Production and Preparation, NVQ Level 2	This course is achieved by continuous assessment.
National Licensees Certificate	This one-day course is suitable for those who wish to run licensed premises.
Basic Food Hygiene Certificate	This is an essential course for anyone who wishes to work in the catering industry.

Recalled Text Exam Practice 2 Document 3

Key in the following document exactly as shown except for line endings which must be allowed to occur naturally. Use a line length of 16cm. Use single-line spacing and a ragged right-hand margin. Save as FOOD3.

FOOD HYGIENE

It is important that all food is handled carefully keeping in mind some basic hygiene rules.

General Hygiene

In order to ensure basic hygiene in the kitchen you should always follow these basic rules:

Wash your hands thoroughly before handling food.
Ensure the work surfaces and utensils are sparkling clean and are washed in hot, soapy water.
Use separate chopping boards for raw and cooked foods.

Refrigeration

Most people now own a refrigerator and/or freezer. These are very effective in preventing the growth of bacteria.

Once purchased, chilled or frozen food should be taken from the shop to your refrigerator as quickly as possible to prevent the food from warming (which allows bacteria to spread).

It is worth investing in a suitable thermometer to check that the refrigerator is working correctly.

The position of the refrigerator is also important. If at all possible it should be positioned away from the cooker.

A good basic kitchen design is as follows:

The position of the food on the shelves should also be taken into consideration. Food should be covered, especially fresh food and liquids. This will help prevent contamination and transference of smells. Place raw foods – especially meat and fish – on the lower shelves. This will stop drips contaminating other foods. It is particularly important that you avoid storing raw and cooked meats together on the same shelf.

Cooking Food

It is important to cook food thoroughly at the correct temperature to ensure bacteria is killed. Food should always be served piping hot.

An oven thermometer can be a good investment as the temperature should be checked regularly to ensure the oven is performing properly.

Cooking times for food – especially raw meat such as poultry – should be calculated accurately.

Recalled Text Exam Practice 2 Document 4

Key in the following document exactly as shown except for line endings which must be allowed to occur naturally. Use a two-column (table) layout for the employment details. Use single-line spacing and a ragged right-hand margin. Save as FOOD4.

Employment Opportunities in Hospitality and Catering

Given below are a few of the jobs we have on offer in the hospitality and catering industry. If you would like to apply for any of these positions, please call

Hotels	
HT12	GENERAL KITCHEN ASSISTANT required at busy town-centre hotel. Applicant must hold a Basic Food Hygiene Certificate. £3.90 per hour
HT22	HEAD CHEF required to lead creative and dynamic team. Small hotel in town-centre location. Salary negotiable.
HT25	RESTAURANT MANAGER required for busy restaurant. Applicants should hold a minimum of HND in Hotel, Catering and Industrial Operations. Salary in the range of £18,000 – £20,000.
Restaurants	
RT8	GENERAL KITCHEN ASSISTANT required for small restaurant in town centre. Three evenings per week, 5.30 pm – 11.30 pm. Transport home provided. £3.75 per hour
RT11	VEGETARIAN CHEF required for a local vegetarian restaurant. Must be committed to serving delicious meals without meat. £15,000+
RT49	WINE WAITER required for luxury restaurant, town-centre location. Applicants must hold relevant qualifications. Excellent salary.
Miscellaneous	
M33	CHEF ASSISTANTS required for fast-food chain. Experience not necessary as full training will be given. Applicants should be enthusiastic and able to work weekends. In excess of £4.10 per hour

These are just a few of the positions we have at present.

Recalled Text Exam Practice 3 Document 1

Key in the following document exactly as shown except for line endings which must be allowed to occur naturally. Save as GARD1.

Valley Garden Centre

Summer Workshops

We are pleased to announce the latest in a series of workshops. These are suitable for both beginners and those with a little experience.

Growing Roses
All you need to know about growing roses.

Planning a Water Garden
Stephen Andrews will give step-by-step instruction on how to design, build and maintain a water garden. Full details on all necessary equipment will be given. All equipment can be purchased at the centre.

Stephen Andrews   £45

Planting a Water Garden
This is a follow-on course to Planning a Water Garden. Stephen gives advice on the best plants available for your garden, how and when to plant and the necessary maintenance required.

Stephen Andrews   £45

Recalled Text Exam Practice 3 Document 3

Key in the following document exactly as shown except for line endings which must be allowed to occur naturally. Use single-line spacing and a ragged right-hand margin. The line length should be 16cm. Save as GARD3.

GARDENING FOR BEGINNERS

Soil

Before you start gardening you should find out whether your soil is alkaline or acid. This is governed by the amount of lime contained in the soil. An alkaline soil is rich in lime or chalk, an acid soil lacks lime. The degree of acidity or alkalinity is measured on the pH scale which runs from 0 to 14.

A soil with a pH value of 7.0 is called neutral. Values over 7.0 are considered alkaline, lower than 7.0 are acidic. Most plants will grow well with a pH value in the range of 6.0 to 7.0.

Simple soil-testing kits are available that will give a rough check on the soil's pH value. You should check this regularly to ensure your soil has not changed.

Climate and Weather

A climate describes a set of conditions prevailing at a given spot over a period. A garden climate depends upon factors such as distance from sea, latitude and winds. A local climate can vary quite widely from the norm of a district. This is called a microclimate.

Plants that will grow in a certain climate are called hardy. This is the resistance to frost and general adaptation to the cycle of seasons in the area. As an example, plants from sub-tropical areas would not be hardy in the UK climate and would need to be protected from cold and frost.

Crop Rotation

If the same crop is grown in the same soil from year to year without feeding, then the soil may lack certain essential nutrients and become prone to disease and pests. Rotating the crops grown each year or so will allow maximum use to be made of the nutrients contained in the soil.

Vegetables are divided into three classes for the purpose of crop rotation. These are shown below:

Each crop requires different nutrients.

Legumes and salads

Root crops

Brassicas

Recalled Text Exam Practice 3 Document 4

Key in the following document exactly as shown except for line endings which must be allowed to occur naturally. Use a two-column (table) layout for the various items. Use single-line spacing and a ragged right-hand margin. Save as GARD4.

Valley Garden Centre

Clematis Promotion

This season we are promoting clematis plants at unbeatable prices.   We have a wide variety of plants in stock. Some of our most popular plants are listed below.

SPRING FLOWERING		
	Markham's Pink Deep-pink double flowers, from mid to late spring. £10.99	£6.99
	Burford White Creamy flowers from early to late spring. £8.99	£7.99
	Apple Blossom Flowers between March and April, wonderful fragrance. £7.99	£6.50
SUMMER FLOWERING		
	Aljonushaka Rich, mauve-pink flowers from July to September. £8.50	£6.99
	Jackmanni One of the most popular plants. Deep-purple flowers appear from June to September. £11.50	£10.00
	Polish Spirit This clematis is suitable for container planting and flowers from midsummer to autumn. Its flowers are rich purple-blue. £9.25	£7.75
AUTUMN FLOWERING		
	Etoile Violette Large flowers which are violet-purple with a reddish tint when young. £4.85	£4.00
	Wyevale This has dark-purple, scented flowers that last from August to October. £7.00	£6.50

WINTER FLOWERING

Wisley Cream This has light-green leaves with greenish-cream flowers. £5.00   £3.50

Ourika Valley This is a hardy plant that has pale-yellow flowers. £8.25   £6.75

Freckles As its name suggests, this has heavily-speckled, creamy-pink flowers. Much prettier than the description. £9.00   £7.75

You will find many more varieties in our nursery. However, if you would like a particular species then we can order it for you.

Recalled Text Exam Practice 4 Document 1

Key in the following document exactly as shown except for line endings which must be allowed to occur naturally. Save as CRAFT1.

CRAFT MONTHLY

Craft Monthly is a specialist magazine featuring all types of craft work.

step-by-step guides
patterns and scale drawings for craft projects

The October issue of Craft Monthly has the first of a 6-part series on ceramics. This special supplement tells you all you need to know to start this fascinating hobby or to improve your existing skills.

Recalled Text Exam Practice 4 Document 3

Key in the following document exactly as shown except for line endings which must be allowed to occur naturally. Use single-line spacing and a ragged right-hand margin. The line length should be 13.5cm and you should use a size 12 font. Save as CRAFT3.

Guide to Ceramics Part I

The basic materials used for the manufacture of ceramics are clay and kaolin. According to composition, use, firing, temperature and deformation in fire, they can be classified as various types of clay. These are:

brick
earthenware
porous (whiteware)
stoneware
porcelain.

Plastic Materials

These are fine-ground rocks formed by clay materials whose particles are less than 2mm in size. The basic property of these materials is their ability, when mixed with water, to form a mouldable body. It does not develop cracks when bent, and retains its shape when dried and fired.

However, a ceramic body composed only of plastic materials would also have its drawbacks. These include shrinkage and poor drying. In order to overcome these problems, Grog and fluxes are added to the basic composition.

Primary Clays

These are a mixture of clay minerals according to the exact composition of the parent rock and its means of decomposition.

Secondary Clays

These are materials that have been transported from the original site of formation. The main agent of transportation is water, however, wind- and glacier-borne clays have been known.

Fireclays

These withstand very high temperatures

Other secondary clays include stoneware, earthenware, brick, Marls and Bentonitic.

Ceramic Batches

Most clays need to be processed before use. Once prepared the ceramic batch should be easy to shape, have low shrinkage and keep its shape when fired. More information on processing will be given later in the series.

Testing

Testing your ceramic materials before use is essential. This will also be featured fully in the series. However, as an example, we will look at the shrinkage test.

First of all make a bar from the ceramic material and mark a precise line, 10cm will be sufficient. See Fig. 1.

The resulting figure is the percentage of shrinkage. This should not exceed 8–10%.

Recalled Text Exam Practice 4 Document 4

Key in the following document exactly as shown except for line endings which must be allowed to occur naturally. Use a four-column (table) layout for the various items. Use single-line spacing and a ragged right-hand margin. Save as CRAFT4.

CLASSIFIED ADVERTISEMENTS

The advertisements listed below have been booked for the September Ceramic Supplement. The copy and rough drafts have already been sent to the designer for pasting up.

COPY	CONTACT NAME	SIZE	PRICE
Exeter Ceramics We can supply all types of clay, glazes, tools and equipment. Competitive prices and free delivery within the Exeter area. (Ceramic Suppliers)	Duncan MacDonald	¼ page	£450
Vinton Ltd Suppliers of raw materials for all types of glazes. Trade enquiries only. For full details call 01721 564632. (Glaze Specialists)	Lorraine Swift	⅛ page	£250
Carlton Pottery If you are interested in learning more about this fascinating craft, then try one of our courses. We offer day, evening, weekend and residential courses. Suitable for beginners and improvers. For further information on our wide range of courses, call 0138 2839183. (Specialist Courses)	Peter Ellesmere	Full page	£2000
Children's Pottery Our pottery workshops are very popular with children aged 8 to 14. Classes are limited to 5 children and cost £45 for a 3-hour session. All materials are provided although children will need to bring protective clothing. Courses held each day during the school holidays. To book a place telephone 01813 2837162. (Bath area). (General Courses)	Margaret Seymour	Full page	£1800

Recalled Text Exam Practice 5 Document 1

Key in the following document exactly as shown except for line endings which must be allowed to occur naturally. Save as CRUISE1.

In association with

The Preferred Travel Company
Bath Branch

Invite you to a cruise evening
on

21 May

at

The Preferred Travel Company,

8.00 pm
Video presentation

8.30 pm
Refreshments

9.00 pm
An opportunity to ask questions

Special deals available for customers who book a holiday at the event.

Recalled Text Exam Practice 5 Document 3

Key in the following document exactly as shown except for line endings which must be allowed to occur naturally. Use single-line spacing and a ragged right-hand margin. The line length should be 14cm. Save as CRUISE3.

CRUISING HOLIDAYS

Taking a cruise may seem to many of us to be beyond our budget. However, this is not the case.

British holidaymakers are beginning to realise the enjoyment that can be had on a cruise. Approximately 650,000 British people took a cruise holiday in 1997 compared with 298,000 in 1993.

Cost

The price of a 7-day cruise can cost as little as £500 per person.

Entertainment

These days most cruises offer plenty of opportunity to visit new places by having a well-planned itinerary. For the few days you are confined on board the liner there are plenty of activities on offer. You can take your pick from gymnasiums, theatres, cinemas, health and beauty treatments, deck sports, lectures and swimming.

Activity Cruises

If you enjoy an active holiday or like to learn new skills, then why not combine these with a cruise? There are many different cruises available which combine both. The activities on offer include creative writing, painting, health and beauty, rock and roll – something to suit all tastes.

Destinations

You can take a cruise to almost anywhere. Many companies offer a two-part holiday. This gives you the opportunity to spend half your holiday at sea and the rest at a hotel.

The length of the cruise varies enormously from a three-day break to a worldwide cruise lasting several months.

Accommodation

There is a wide choice of accommodation on board most liners. This generally ranges from a small cabin with private bathroom to large suites, which include a sitting room, bedroom and bathroom. Outside cabins – those, which are facing the sea – cost more than inside cabins. Inside cabins do not have a sea view.

Food and Drink

You will certainly eat well on your holiday. Many tours offer 6 meals each day – some even offer 8.

A typical day's meals would include:

full breakfast
elevenses
three-course buffet lunch.

Recalled Text Exam Practice 5 Document 4

Key in the following document exactly as shown except for line endings which must be allowed to occur naturally. Use a three-column (table) layout for the various items. Use single-line spacing and a ragged right-hand margin. Save as CRUISE4.

June Vacations

SHIP	DETAILS	PRICE PER PERSON FROM
St Lucia	Fly to Orlando and meet your ship at Fort Lauderdale. The ship docks at Nassau, San Juan, St John and St Thomas, Half Moon Cay returning to Fort Lauderdale. Return flight from Orlando. 7 nights	£750
Fiesta	This cruise offers a variety of cities, islands and beaches to ensure you enjoy the best of the Carribean. You can enjoy shopping in some of the great cities followed by exploring unspoilt islands. 10 nights	£1450
President	Our Italian cruise is excellent value for money. It is a 7-night cruise but can be extended with a 7-night stay on land.	£720 or
	Fly to Palma to join the President. The ship calls at Rome, Naples, Messina (Sicily), Malta and Sardinia. You then return to Palma for your flight home or to transfer to your chosen accommodation. 7 or 14 nights	£1300
Maria	Our second Caribbean cruise has a different route but is equally exciting. This cruise can be combined with a 7-night stay on land.	£595 or
		£1100

Recalled Text Exam Practice 6 Document 1

Key in the following document exactly as shown except for line endings which must be allowed to occur naturally. Save as LIFE1.

LIFE STYLE MAGAZINE

The third edition

All you need to know – the latest ideas and articles on

Keeping Fit
Sports, equipment, exercise

Looking Good
The latest in fashion, make-up, hair and style

Feeling Great
Healthy recipes

Features on:

hay fever
stress
dieting
the most fashionable places to holiday

Price £2.75
Order a copy from your newsagent now!

Everything you need to keep you looking good and feeling great

Make-up advice for a natural-looking summer

Recalled Text Exam Practice 6 Document 3

Key in the following document exactly as shown except for line endings which must be allowed to occur naturally. Use a line length of 16cm. Use single-line spacing and a ragged right-hand margin. Save as LIFE3.

Healthy Eating

In the past the most usual way to calculate if you were overweight was to use a weight table. However, this is not the most accurate method, as it does not take into account various other factors such as your build or frame.

The recommended way to calculate your body weight is the Body Mass Index (BMI). It is calculated by dividing the weight in kilograms by the square of the height in metres.

The final figure is your BMI and you compare it to the following:

BMI 20 or below – Underweight
BMI 20 – 24.9 – Normal
BMI 25 – 29.9 – Plump

If your calculation tells you that you have a BMI of 25 or over then you may wish to lose some weight. It is very important that you consult your GP before entering into any type of diet.

If you do have to lose some weight then adopt a sensible eating plan. You must include plenty of fresh vegetables and salads, together with protein and fibre-giving foods such as meat, bread, fish, cheese, etc.

<u>Vitamins and Minerals</u>

<u>Carbohydrates</u>

These are essential energy-giving foods. Although most carbohydrates are good for us, foods high in sugar should be eaten in moderation.

<u>Fats</u>

These are also energy-giving foods but, because of their high cholesterol and calorie values, should be eaten in moderation. These foods include butter, margarine, cooking oil, some processed foods such as crisps and foods that have been fried.

<u>Proteins</u>

Milk, eggs, cheese, fish, pulses and nuts all contain proteins. These are body-building foods that assist growth and repair damaged tissue.

Recalled Text Exam Practice 6 Document 4

Key in the following document exactly as shown except for line endings which must be allowed to occur naturally. Use a two-column (table) layout, single-line spacing and a ragged right-hand margin. Save as LIFE4.

The Most Fashionable Hairdressers

Our intrepid reporter Frances Page was sent to investigate some of the most fashionable hairdressers. As she feels her hair is already perfect she asked four testers to have various treatments. Here are the results. The star rating is 5 = excellent, 1 = poor.

EUGÈNE LONDON	The tester, Louise decided to go for a complete restyle of her shoulder-length blonde hair. Clutching a photo of an unsuitable style she ventured in. ****
JOHN AND JANE MANCHESTER	Kathy was our tester in Manchester. She decided to have a restyle and blonde highlights put through her rather mousy-coloured hair. Kathy mentioned this when booking the appointment and was asked to have a consultation prior to the appointment. *****
GREENS LEEDS	Roberta booked an appointment for her long hair to be styled for a special night out. She explained to the stylist how she wanted her hair to look and sat back to relax. One hour later she emerged feeling happy with the result but extremely unhappy with the price of £55.
HEAD MASTERS BRISTOL	Suzy tested this fairly new hairdressers. Suzy already has a perm and colour on her hair but decided to try highlights as well. She booked an appointment with Peter, a senior stylist. When Suzy complained, she was treated in an off-hand manner and the manager would not reduce the fee of £65. *

Recalled Text Exam Practice 7 Document 1

Key in the following document exactly as shown except for line endings which must be allowed to occur naturally. Save as FRANCH1.

Are you fed up with working for someone else?

Would you like to be your own boss?

Find out more at the

Franchising is the modern way to start a business as many of the usual risks have been eliminated.

Your initial investment may be as little as £5,000.

We will be offering the following workshops for those interested in franching.

Saturday   Service Industry
11.00 am

Saturday   Commercial Cleaning
2.00 am

Recalled Text Exam Practice 7 Document 3

Key in the following document exactly as shown except for line endings which must be allowed to occur naturally. Use a line length of 16cm, single-line spacing and a ragged right-hand margin. Save as FRANCH3.

Business Franchising

What is Franchising?

Franchising in its most basic form is an arrangement between one party, the franchisor, who has a blueprint and system for a business, and a second party who wishes to copy the business.

The franchisor – the person or company with the idea and system – should have developed a tested blueprint for a successful business. They will have tested the market, developed the product or service and attained the skills necessary to make the business a success.

What are the Benefits of Franchising?

As previously mentioned, the franchisee should be given full training in the business and be able to ask for help when needed.

Some franchisors offer their franchisees an exclusive area so that competition is limited. It is of course in the franchisor's interests to have successful franchisees.

What do I Need to Start my own Business?

In order to make a success of your business you will need the following:

Capital. As well as your initial investment you will also need money to live on while you are setting up your business.

Time and effort. Running your own business takes a great deal of time and effort, especially when you first start. If you wish to work nine to five, five days a week, then maybe you are not suited to running a business.

Experience. Many franchisees have not had previous experience in running a business in their market area.

What are the Drawbacks of Franchising?

You must put in a great deal of time and effort on building up your business. This means long hours, often unsociable. This can often put a strain on family life, so you will need support and often practical help from your friends and family.

As the franchisor may take a percentage of your turnover, you will need to generate a larger turnover in order to provide an income.

For example, if the franchise agreement states that you must pay, say 3% of your turnover in fees, you will need to increase turnover by approximately 5% in order to achieve the same level of success as a non-franchised business.

Recalled Text Exam Practice 7 Document 4

Key in the following document exactly as shown except for line endings which must be allowed to occur naturally. Use a two-column (table) layout, single-line spacing and a ragged right-hand margin. Save as FRANCH4.

Minutes of Meeting of the Exhibition Committee

Held on 21 October

Present: Lyon, Laurence Brady, Hamish Grant

Apologies: Michael Read, Paul Douglas

1 MINUTES OF LAST MEETING	These were agreed and signed.
2 MATTERS ARISING	Booking of conference centre. DR confirmed that the conference centre has accepted our booking and that all services requested can be provided.
4 ADVERTISING 4.1 Trade Stands	This was talked about at some length. Invitations to book stands will be sent to all regular exhibitors. New franchisees will also be invited. These must go out within the next few weeks in order to maximise bookings. Overseas companies should be faxed before the end of the month.
	Once CL has calculated the break-even point the intensity of the advertising can be discussed. (Action CL)
4.2 Visitors	This will be delayed until the required no. of bookings has been made.
5 PRINTING	The printing of information packs for traders can now be confirmed. It is anticipated that approx. 800 will be required. After some discussion, it was agreed the contract for printing should be given to Marshall & Co. LB to make the final arrangements. (Action LB)
6 SECURITY	The conference centre confirmed that they can provide all necessary security personnel if required. This is at a cost of £1800 per day. DR to consider alternative arrangements. (Action DR)
7 ANY OTHER BUSINESS	There were no other matters arising.
8 DATE OF NEXT MEETING	This will be held on 20 December in the conference room at 2.30 pm.
	The meeting closed at 5.00 pm.

Recalled Text Exam Practice 8 Document 1

Key in the following document exactly as shown except for line endings which must be allowed to occur naturally. Save as DECOR1.

Life Style Magazine

AGENDA AND NOTES FOR CHAIR

1   APOLOGIES

2   MINUTES OF PREVIOUS MEETING

3   MATTERS ARISING Check that Lorraine Dyer has confirmed the booking of a house at St Ives for the Christmas on the Beach feature.

4   JULY CAR BOOT BARGAINS

6   DATE OF NEXT MEETING

Recalled Text Exam Practice 8 Document 3

Key in the following document exactly as shown except for line endings which must be allowed to occur naturally. Use a ragged right-hand margin, a line length of 14cm and single-line spacing. Save as DECOR3.

HOME DECORATION

Calculating the Materials Required

If you are going to decorate a room you will need to work out the amount of materials required.

It is important that you purchase the correct amount before you start work as the shades of paint and wallpapers may vary slightly from batch to batch. Different types of paint such as emulsion or gloss will cover different areas depending on its consistency. Your local Do-It-Yourself store will be able to give advice on this.

Paint

As stated above, paint shades can vary from batch to batch, so it is important to purchase the necessary quantity before starting to paint. As a general rule a standard tin will contain one litre of paint. To decide how much paint to buy, calculate the area to be painted by multiplying the height by the width of each wall and then add all the totals together.

To calculate the paint needed for moulded window or door frames, multiply the height by the width of the frames and consider it as a solid surface.

To paint a moulded door, multiply the height of the door by the width and add one quarter to allow for the increased surface area caused by the moulding.

Types of Paint

There are many different types of paint available, and most have a specific use, for example, paints for wood, walls, pipes, timber and guttering. You will need to find out the type of paint most suitable for the surface you are covering.

The amount of paint you buy will depend on many factors. For example, you will need to buy more paint if any of the following apply:

the type of paint being used is particularly porous
if the area being covered is textured
if you are painting over a dark colour

Once you have calculated the room measurements you should be able to obtain advice from your local Do-It-Yourself store on how much paint will be required, bearing in mind the factors given above.

As well as these factors, keep in mind that different types of paint will cover different amounts of surface area.

Recalled Text Exam Practice 8 Document 4

Key in the following document exactly as shown except for line endings which must be allowed to occur naturally. Use a two-column (table) layout for the various items. Use single-line spacing and a ragged right-hand margin. Save as DECOR4.

COLOUR SCHEMES

It can be difficult choosing a colour scheme that is right for your home.

Bedroom

COOL BLUE	Try a cool blue bedroom using bluebell paint for walls with a crisp white for doors, skirtings and ceilings. The Country Flowers range by Hilton-Smith Designs contains a variety of bedlinen, wallpapers and curtains that would complement this colour scheme. Hilton-Smith 0121 2882919

Living Room

MELLOW YELLOW	Pale lemon gives a warm and light feel to any room. In fact lemon can make a room seem lighter than white. It is a good contrast to many other colours. The best range of lemon and yellow paints can be found at Pierre Pelletier. Pierre Pelletier 0927 451308

Kitchen

COFFEE EXPRESSO	For a fashionable, stylish look try lots of stainless steel. Many appliances are now available with a steel finish, or you can achieve the effect with smaller electrical appliances such as toasters and kettles. This look needs a minimalist approach, so if you like lots of clutter then it may not be right for your home. The Lotus chain has the best range of steel accessories on the market. Lotus 0139 493987

Document Presentation

The Stage III Document Presentation Part II examination offered by RSA Examinations Board tests your ability to key in and lay out four business documents from handwritten and typewritten drafts as well as recalled text. You will need to use a word processor to complete the examination.

You will be asked to type and amend four documents in one and three-quarter hours. These are:

1 document incorporating an element of design
2 a document incorporating a variety of column styles and fonts
3 a multi-page technical document incorporating a diagram
4 a multi-column, multi-page document.

You will be asked to use a house style for two of the documents. These are given on a reference sheet at the back of the examination paper. Remember that the information printed there is for reference only, do not type in the text shown.

You should ensure that second and subsequent pages of a document are numbered. Remember to read the instructions carefully to find out the page number you must start numbering from. In order to pass the examination you must complete the paper within the time given and incur no more than 14 faults. If you incur 5 or less, you will be awarded a distinction.

Three of the tasks in this examination include text that has previously been keyed in by your tutor. The examination requires you to recall these files and make amendments as instructed.

The text which needs to be keyed in for the purpose of the document presentation mock examination papers in this book can be found on pages 9–35.

If you are drawing a diagram then ensure that all lines touch each other but do not overlap. Try to make your diagrams as neat as possible. The diagram which must be reproduced and inserted can be found on the reference sheet.

Remember to add all necessary text boxes and to shade boxes as appropriate. Borders and dividers must not be forgotten and should not touch any existing text.

If you are typing accents, fractions or mathematical symbols, do check that you have used the correct symbol. Go through these character by character, especially if some of the symbols you are typing have to be displayed as either subscript or superscript characters.

When instructed, you must ensure that you have printed a header and/or footer on each page using the correct font sizes specified.

One problem candidates face is running out of time in the examination. Not only must you complete the examination paper but you should also have enough time left to check your work carefully. When you are working through the mock examination papers in this section you may like to make a note of the time each document has taken. As a guide you should aim to complete the tasks within the following time scale:

- Document 1 – 20 minutes.
- Document 2 – 15 minutes.
- Document 3 – 25 minutes.
- Document 4 – 30 minutes.

This will allow you a total of 15 minutes to read the instructions before you type and to check through your work on completion.

Exam Practice 1 Document 1

Recall this document stored as HOME1. Display it as indicated on the Reference Sheet, and amend it as shown. Save as HOME1A and print one copy.

HAVE YOU EVER WISHED YOU COULD BUILD YOUR OWN HOME?

you can!

Add a full page border

MANY PEOPLE BUILD THEIR DREAM HOMES EACH YEAR.

how do they do it?

Come along to the Design and Build™ Show at

Sponsored by Design and Build™ Magazine ← Shade this box and use a larger font size

Thousands of people build their own home each year. Building your own home may seem to be an unrealistic dream, but it is achievable. How can you do it? Come and talk to the experts and find out.

Booking details can be found on http://DesignBuild.com.uk

We will be holding workshops on:

Timber-framed houses
Finding a suitable building plot
How to budget for the build
How to calculate the quantity of materials required.

Use bullet points and a different font size and style for this section.

Insert a text box here 10cm wide × 3cm high with the words

The Angel Hotel
LEEDS
Friday, Saturday and Sunday
20 - 22 November
9.00 am - 4.00pm.
Centre the text box on the page and Centre the words within it.

Advance tickets
Adults — £5
Accompanied children under 16 years - Free

Key in using a consistent typeface and layout. Save as HOME2 and print on one side of a sheet of A4 paper.

Emphasise this heading

Building Measurements

Add a clip-art picture here

The Imperial system of measurement
used in Britain for many years evolved
over the centuries. Many of these were
measured by parts of the body.

*For example, a yard was the distance from the nose to the end
of an outstretched arm. Obviously, this method was not
always accurate.*

The French introduced the metric system based on more standard
measures.

NAPOLEON INTRODUCED THIS SYSTEM WHEREVER HE ESTABLISHED HIS
EMPIRE.

Use a two-column layout for this section

Over the years there has been a number of attempts to bring Britain's
measuring system into line with other European countries.

However, it was not until 1976 that the Weights and Measures Act gave the
Government permission to phase out Imperial measurements.

*The system gradually being introduced into Britain today
is the Système Internationale d'Unités, often abbreviated
to SI.*

The main advantage of this system is that there is a symbol for each
unit. This means that it does not need to be translated into
any language.

**Although exact conversion figures
exist to change Imperial measure
into metric, many of these figures
include several decimal points.**

*Insert horizontal
dividers at places
marked ——H——*

To make conversion easier, figures are
often rounded up or down to the nearest
whole number or 0.5 (½).

Exam Practice 1 Document 3

Recall this document stored as HOME3. Insert a header BUYING LAND at the top right margin and a footer Article 17 32₄46 at the right margin using a point 8 font for both. Number the pages at the bottom left starting with page 10. Adjust the line length to 11cm and use full justification. Save as HOME3A and print one copy using double-line spacing except where indicated.

Choosing a suitable site ← Centre this heading

Insert this paragraph 25mm from both margins

Although building your own home is a realistic dream, finding the right site can be a frustrating and time-consuming process. However, it is extremely important that you take the time to check out building sites thoroughly for their suitability. Cutting corners when purchasing a site can mean a lot of time and money later on.

Measuring the Site

When you find a potential building site, walk round it checking the boundaries and measurements. Ensure they are the same as on the sale details, the deeds and any planning permission. If a discrepancy comes to light you will have to call the vendor, agent and solicitor to work out the correct details.

As a rough guide, to find the total area of the site make the following calculation: $l \times b = m^2$. If the area is not rectangular, but circular, the calculation is πr^2.

Insert diagram from reference sheet here.

This will give you the total site area. Remember that the proposed dwelling must fit easily onto the site including access for your vehicles.

Site Problems

Use single-line spacing for this paragraph

existing foundations

Check the site for possible problems. These may include ponds, trees, ~~areas of concrete,~~ ditches, etc. Assess whether you can deal with these easily or whether they will add thousands of pounds to your building budget. Wet areas or a spring can also cause problems on the site. However, in dry weather, these may not be obvious immediately. Indicators can be willows, rushes or alders, ~~although you should not jump to conclusions~~.

Exam Practice 1 Document 3 ctd

Services

If the land already has the main services connected (these are sewerage, gas, water and electricity) check the position of the various manholes, stopcocks and pipes. If these need to be diverted to accommodate your building this could prove expensive.

If there are no existing services check the immediate vicinity to see where they are. Connection fees can be very costly. <u>Bear in mind that you have no automatic right to cross land that does not belong to you in order to connect the services.</u>

Access

Obviously you will need to have ~~adequate~~ Satisfactory access to the site. If you are planning to buy a site on a private road you will need to obtain access rights. ~~This can take time and money.~~ You will also need to ~~be able to~~ have good visibility at the point your drive would join the public highway.

As a rough guide take 2½ paces back from this point and check up and down the road. Hedges, telegraph poles, trees and fences may all block your access.

If any of these problems do ~~come to light~~ arise, your solicitor should be able to give you advice on how to solve them.

Change site to plot throughout this document.

Exam Practice 1 Document 4

Recall this document stored as HOME4 and display as the example on the Reference Sheet. Complete the document. Save as HOME4A and print one copy

Land for Sale

The following plots of land are all suitable for building residential accommodation. For full details, including viewing appointments, please contact Louis François quoting the correct reference number.

COUNTY	PLOT DETAILS	REF NO
Berkshire		
	Grade II listed thatched cottage in need of complete renovation. ~~£100,000~~ £120,000	BK1
	(Add BK2 here)	
Cambridgeshire		
	Four plots each with a site area of ½ acre. Each has outline planning permission for a detached dwelling. £50,000 per plot	CM1
Cheshire	(Add CM2 here)	
	Single building plot with outline planning permission for 3-bedroomed property. £39,000	CH1
	(Add CH2 here)	
Cornwall	(Add CW1 here)	
	Plot measuring 100ft x 63ft with lapsed outline planning permission for a single detached dwelling. The plot is located in a village inland. £5~~8~~9,000	CW2
	Beautiful sea views from this plot measuring $530m^2$. Detailed planning permission for a 2-storey, 3-bedroomed dwelling. £64,000	CW3
Suffolk	Barn	
	~~Chapel~~ suitable for conversion. Total site area ¼ acre with outline planning permission granted. £85,000	SK1
	(Add SK2 here)	
Yorkshire		
	Site for sale totalling 1 acre. Outline planning permission granted for 3 detached, 2-storey dwellings. Owner will split into separate plots. £120,000 or £45,000 per plot.	YK1

Although we have made every effort to ensure the details given are correct, we strongly recommend you consult a solicitor before entering into a contract.

2

(BK2) Building plot, ¼ acre with outline planning permission for 2-storey dwelling. £110,000

(CM2) Range of farm buildings on site of approximately ⅛ acre. Detailed planning permission to convert to pair of semi-detached dwellings. Offers invited.

(CH2) Building plot in central location measuring approximately 49ft × 117ft. Outline planning permission for detached dwelling. £42,000

(CW1) Barn with outbuildings on plot of approximately 1 acre. All services are connected and the plot has detailed planning permission for a 4-bedroomed dwelling. Wonderful sea views. £130,000

(SK2) Derelict bungalow requiring demolition. Planning permission unknown. Site measures ⅓ acre. Offers over £65,000

Exam Practice 1 Reference Sheet

Information on this sheet is not to be copied. It indicates the house style required for the documents.

Document 1

Display the paragraphs and their headings as shown here.

Would you like to design your home to your own specifications?

YOU CAN!

Would you like to build a home for approximately $^1/_3$ less than its market value?

YOU WOULD!

Document 3

Diagram – This does not have to be reproduced in this exact size and can be adjusted to fit the space available in your document. Either squares or rectangles can be used. Use any font size or style.

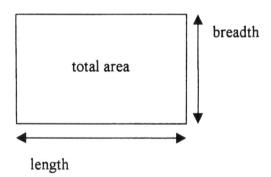

Document 4

Use capitalisation and a four-column layout as in this specimen layout.

COUNTY	PLOT DETAILS	REF NO	PRICE
DYFED	Wonderful ½-acre site just 1 mile from coast. Planning permission for detached dwelling.	DY1	£45,000
SOMERSET	Small plot measuring 44ft x 65ft, in residential area.	SM1	Offers invited

Exam Practice 2 Document 1

Recall this document stored as FOOD1.
Display it as shown on the Reference sheet and amend it as shown. Save as FOOD1A and print one copy.

Would you like to work with lots of people?

Do you enjoy a challenge?

Have you considered a career in catering?

Centre this box + the text within it. Use a shaded box

If so, why not join one of our catering and hospitality courses?

Use a larger font

There lead to professional qualifications that will ensure you have excellent career prospects.

COURSES AVAILABLE

Food Production and Preparation, NVQ Level 2

Course Leader: Héléna Cilèa

This course is ~~achieved~~ *attained* by continuous assessment. It is useful if you already have employment in the catering industry. However, we can arrange a work placement.

National Licensees Certificate

Course Leader: Hans Dvôrák

This one-day course is suitable for those who wish to run licensed premises.

Basic Food Hygiene Certificate

Course Leader: Joan Lovell

This is an essential course for anyone who wishes to work in the catering industry. Successful students may wish to continue their studies through the Intermediate and Advanced Certificates.

Add a full-page border

Insert a text box 8.5cm wide x 3cm high with the words

For further information contact:
Laura Stockwood on 01293 28282 or
e-mail   L.Stockwood@Coll.com
Use a different font size and style

Key in using a consistent typeface and layout. Save as FOOD2 and print on one side of a sheet of A4 paper.

Healthy Eating

This recipe is super for dining al fresco with friends.

A warm summer's evening, some good red wine, crusty bread and a mixed green salad is all that is needed to accompany this dish.

Add a clip-art picture here

Ingredients

4 large aubergines, 300g low-fat mozzarella cheese, 1 jar pesto, 2 tbsps olive oil, ½ litre passata, 2 cloves garlic, 100g cheddar cheese, 1 medium-sized onion, 2 tbsps sun-dried tomato paste, handful chopped basil.

Preparation

Heat the oven to Gas mark 5/190°C/375°F. Slice each aubergine lengthways and brush lightly with the olive oil. Fry until soft.

Spread each slice with a little pesto and then place 2 small slices of mozzarella on top. Roll carefully and place into a greased baking dish.

Repeat with the rest of the aubergine slices.

Now chop and fry the onion and garlic in a heavy-based saucepan until soft. Add the passata, basil and sun-dried tomato paste and heat through.

Pour on top of the aubergine rolls. Sprinkle the grated cheddar cheese on top and bake for 25 – 30 minutes.

Use a two-column layout for this section.

Dessert ideas for this meal include lemon and lime cheesecake, summer fruit sorbet or lemon torte.

Add horizontal dividers at places marked ——//

Bon appetit!

Exam Practice 2 Document 3

Recall this document stored as FOOD3. Insert a header Lecture Notes^12/4 and centre it. Insert a footer © George Knight 1998 at the left-hand margin. Number the pages at the bottom right starting with page 6. Adjust the line length to 12cm and use a justified right hand margin. Use a point 10 font for the header and footer. Print one copy in double-line spacing and save as FOOD3A.

FOOD HYGIENE

It is ~~important~~ essential that all food is handled carefully keeping in mind some basic hygiene rules. This is to prevent bacteria from growing and causing food poisoning.

General Hygiene

In order to ensure basic hygiene in the kitchen you should always follow these basic rules:

Apply bullet points to this section

Wash your hands thoroughly before handling food.
Ensure the work surfaces and utensils are sparkling clean and ~~are~~ have been washed in hot, soapy water.
Use separate chopping boards for raw and cooked foods.

Refrigeration

Most people now own a refrigerator and/or freezer. These are very effective in preventing the growth of bacteria. However, it is important that food is stored correctly and that the appliance is working at the correct temperature.

Once purchased, chilled or frozen food should be ~~taken~~ transferred from the shop to your refrigerator as quickly as possible to prevent the food from warming (which allows bacteria to spread).

Once the food is in the refrigerator, it should be stored at the correct temperature. A domestic refrigerator should have a temperature of $\leq 4°C$ at all times. This is because food poisoning organisms will grow at temperatures of $\geq 5°C$ in a refrigerator or $-15°C$ in a freezer.

Exam Practice 2 Document 3 ctd

If your kitchen is hot, and this applies particularly in warm weather, you may need to adjust the thermostat accordingly.

It is worth investing in a suitable thermometer to check that the refrigerator is working correctly.

The position of the refrigerator is also important. If at all possible it should be positioned away from the cooker. *It should have a space of at least 50mm from the wall to allow heat to escape.*

A good basic kitchen design is as follows:

Copy diagram from Reference sheet here

This paragraph in Single-line spacing

The position of the food on the shelves should also be taken into consideration. Food should be covered, especially fresh food and liquids. This will help prevent contamination and transference of smells. Place raw foods – especially meat and fish – on the lower shelves. This will stop drips contaminating other foods. It is particularly important that you avoid storing raw and cooked meats together on the same shelf.

Cooking Food

Inset this Section 20 mm from both margins

It is important to cook food thoroughly at the correct temperature to ensure bacteria is killed. Food should always be served piping hot.

An oven thermometer can be a good investment as the temperature should be checked regularly to ensure the oven is performing properly. *Remember, if you are cooking two or more dishes at the same time, the cooking time may need to be extended.*

Exam Practice 2 Document 3 ctd

Cooking times for food – especially raw meat such as poultry – should be calculated accurately. For example, a turkey will need to be cooked for 20 mins per pound in weight, plus an extra 20 mins. The calculation you will need to make is:

$$(b \times c) + c \quad (\text{where } c = 20 \text{ mins} + b = \text{weight in pounds}).$$

Exam Practice 2 Document 4

Recall this document stored as FOOD4 and display as the example on the Reference sheet. Complete the document and print one copy. Save as FOOD4A.

Employment Opportunities in Hospitality and Catering

Given below are a few of the jobs we have on offer in the hospitality and catering industry. If you would like to apply for any of these positions, please call *Hannah Parslow on 01344 5277612 and quote the appropriate reference number.*

Hotels

HT12   GENERAL KITCHEN ASSISTANT required at busy town-centre hotel. Applicant must hold a Basic Food Hygiene Certificate. ~~£3.90~~ per hour *£4.10*

Add HT14 here

HT22   HEAD CHEF required to lead ~~creative and dynamic~~ team. Small hotel in town-centre location. Salary negotiable.

HT25   RESTAURANT MANAGER required for busy *hotel* restaurant. Applicants should hold a minimum of HND in Hotel, Catering and Industrial Operations. Salary in the range of £18,000 – £20,000.

Restaurants

Add RT14 here

RT8   GENERAL KITCHEN ASSISTANT required for small restaurant in town centre. ~~Three~~ *Four* evenings per week, 5.30 pm – 11.30 pm. Transport home provided. £3.75 per hour

RT~~H~~ 21   VEGETARIAN CHEF required for a local vegetarian restaurant. Must be committed to serving delicious meals without meat. £15,000+

Add RT43 here

RT49   WINE WAITER required for ~~luxury~~ *award-winning* restaurant, town-centre location. Applicants must hold relevant qualifications. Excellent salary.

Miscellaneous

M33   ~~CHEF~~ *CATERING* ASSISTANTS required for fast-food chain. Experience not necessary as full training will be given. Applicants should be enthusiastic and able to work weekends. In excess of £4.10 per hour

Add M37 here

These are just a few of the positions we have at present. *To find out more browse our website http//jobs@HCI.com.*

Change town to City throughout this document

(HT14) WAITING STAFF large country house hotel requires trained and experienced silver service staff. Hours 6.00pm – midnight, five evenings per week to include Saturdays. Own transport essential. £4.20 per hour.

(RT4) PATISSIÈRE CHEF required at exclusive restaurant situated on outskirts of town. Applicants should hold all relevant qualifications and have had at least three years' experience. Salary negotiable.

(RT43) WAITING STAFF required for small, friendly restaurant. No experience required as full training will be given. £3.40 per hour.

(M37) CATERING ASSISTANTS required for local hospital. Applicants should NVQ level 2 in catering. £3.95 per hour.

Exam Practice 2 Reference Sheet

Information on this sheet is not to be copied. It indicates the house style required for the documents.

Document 1

Display the paragraphs and their headings as shown here.

<u>Cake Decoration – Intermediate</u>

A follow-on course. Students must attain the introductory Certificate before enrolling on this course.

Course Leader: Karen Westerly

<u>Pastry Studies – Advanced</u>

This course will teach you patissière skills using base pastes, yeast, etc.

Course Leader: Laurence Willis

Document 3

Diagram – This does not have to be reproduced in this exact size and can be adjusted to fit the space available in your document. Either squares or rectangles can be used. Use any font size or style.

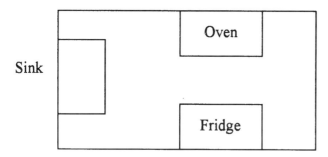

Document 4

Use capitalisation and a three-column layout as in this specimen layout.

CAFES

CF13	<u>Waiting Staff</u> required for small, busy café. Must be able to work weekends.	£3.80 per hour
CF18	<u>Cashier</u> required at town-centre café. This is a full-time position, Monday – Friday.	£3.95 per hour

Exam Practice 3 Document 1

Recall this document stored as GARD1. Display it as indicated on the Reference Sheet and amend it as shown. Save as GARD1A and print one copy.

Valley Garden Centre ← Use a larger font size and shade this box

Summer workshops ← Emphasise and centre this heading

We are pleased to announce the latest in a series of workshops. These are suitable for both beginners and those with a little experience.

Monday 2 May 10.00 am – 12 noon	**Growing Roses** All you need to know about growing roses. Whether you wish to grow patio, climber or standard roses. When to plant, the varieties available, pruning etc. Delorés O'Sullivan £15
Tuesday 3 May 10.00 am – 4.00 pm	Planning a water garden Stephen Andrews will give step by step instruction on how to design, build and maintain a water garden. Full details on all necessary equipment will be given. ~~All equipment can be purchased at the Centre.~~ Stephen Andrews £45
Tuesday 10 May 10.00 am – 4.00 pm	Planting a water garden This is a follow-on course to Planning a water garden. Stephen gives advice on the best plants available for your garden, how and when to plant and the necessary maintenance ~~required.~~ Stephen Andrews £45

Insert a text box in the centre 12 cm wide and 3 cm high, with the words:

Call Zoë Greening on
01231   928726
for enrolment details

Use a different font size and style and Centre the words within the text box.

Add a full-page border

Key in using a consistent typeface and layout. Save as GARD2 and print on one side of a sheet of A4 paper.

Growing Roses

Add a clip-art picture here.

There are over 500 different varieties of roses. How do you choose which plant will be suitable for you? Follow our handy guide given below:

———————— ✕ ————————

Use a two-column layout for this section

Full Sun

Some plants fade in strong sunlight. To avoid this try Rouge Cardinal or Ernest Markham.

Both of these grow to approximately 3m and flower from midsummer to early autumn.

Shade

If you have shady areas in your garden then try Blue Moon.

This new variety has large white flowers suffused with pale lilac. It grows to a height of 2½m.

Another variety that is happiest in shade is Blue Belle. This deep violet-purple flowering plant grows to approximately 3¼m. It flowers from July to September.

Change roses to Clematis throughout this document

Ground Cover

To cover patches of ground try this sprawling variety. Pagoda produces creamy pink-mauve flowers from early to late summer and is happy in sun or shade.

It is a very hardy plant and grows to a height of 3m.

———————— ✕ ————————

These are just a few of the roses that can work well in your garden. There are also varieties that are particularly suitable for growing in containers.

If you require scented flowers, there are a large number of fragrant plants to choose from. Ask our experienced staff for help and advice.

Insert horizontal dividers at places marked ——➤✕

Recall this draft stored as GARD3 . Insert a header GARDENING HINTS AND TIPS at the right-hand margin and a footer Series 1 © John Daniels in the centre using a point 10 font for both. Number the pages at the top left starting with page 3. Adjust the line length to 12 cm and use full justification and a size 12 font. Save as GARD3A and print one copy in treble-line spacing except where indicated.

GARDENING FOR BEGINNERS

Soil

Inset this paragraph by 25 mm from both margins

Before you start gardening you should find out whether your soil is alkaline or acid. This is governed by the amount of lime contained in the soil. An alkaline soil is rich in lime or chalk, an acid soil lacks lime. The degree of acidity or alkalinity is measured on the pH scale which runs from 0 to 14. The pH is the negative logarithm to base 10 of H^+ ion concentration, calculated using the following formula: $pH = log_{10}(1/(H^+))$.

A soil with a pH value of 7.0 is called neutral. Values over 7.0 are considered alkaline, lower than 7.0 are acidic. Most plants will grow well with a pH value in the range of 6.0 to 7.0.

Simple soil-testing kits are available that will ~~give a rough~~ check ~~on~~ the soil's pH value. You should ~~check~~ test this regularly ~~to ensure your soil has not changed~~.

Climate and Weather

Use single-line spacing for these paragraphs

A climate describes a set of conditions prevailing at a given spot over a period. A garden climate depends upon factors such as distance from sea, latitude and winds. A local climate can vary quite widely from the norm of a district. This is called a microclimate.

Plants that will grow in a certain climate are called hardy. This is the resistance to frost and general adaptation to the cycle of seasons in the area. As an example, plants from sub-tropical areas would not be hardy in the UK climate and would need to be protected from cold and frost.

The growing season is defined as the number of days the temperature rises above 6°C (43°F) which is the temperature at which grass begins to grow. Land is divided into zones of growth and Europe varies from zone 2 - which has only 150 growing days per year - to zone 10 - where growth is continuous.

Exam Practice 3 Document 3 ctd

Crop Rotation

If the same crop is grown in the same soil from year to year without feeding, then the soil may lack certain essential nutrients and become prone to disease and pests. Rotating the crops grown each year or so will allow maximum use to be made of the nutrients contained in the soil.

Vegetables are divided into three classes for the purpose of crop rotation. These are shown below:

Insert here the diagram shown on the reference sheet. You may use squares or rectangles.

Each crop requires different nutrients.

Use bullet points for these 3 paragraphs

Legumes and salads will require a more alkaline soil and therefore lime may need to be added during the winter months. Approximately three weeks before planting apply fertilizer at a rate of 55g/m². To calculate this use the formula m² x 55g.

Root crops will need fertilizer applied at 110g/m²

Brassicas will need 170 – 220g/m² of lime if the soil has a pH value of >6.5.

Therefore, for an area measuring 2 m² x 4 m² which is to be planted with legumes, the calculation will be 8 m² x 55g = 460 g.

Recall this document stored as GARD4 and display as the example on the Reference sheet. Complete the document. Save as GARD4A and print one copy.

Valley Garden Centre

Clematis Promotion

This season we are promoting clematis plants at unbeatable prices.   We have a wide variety of plants in stock. Some of our most popular plants are listed below.

Add these column headings

Type	Details	Sale Price	Usual Price
SPRING FLOWERING			
	Markham's Pink Deep-pink double flowers, from ~~mid~~ *early* to late spring. £10.99	£6.99	
	Burford White Creamy flowers from early to late spring. £8.99 *Add Niobe here*	£7.99	
	Apple Blossom Flowers between March and April, wonderful fragrance. ~~£7.99~~ £9.99	£6.50	
SUMMER FLOWERING			
	Aljonushaka Rich, mauve-pink flowers from July to September. £8.50 *Add Summer Snow here*	£6.99	
	Jackmanni One of the most popular plants. Deep-purple flowers appear from June to September. £11.50 *Add Ascotiensus here*	£10.00	
	Polish Spirit This clematis is suitable for container planting and flowers from midsummer to autumn. Its flowers are rich purple-blue. £9.25	~~£7.75~~ £6.50	
AUTUMN FLOWERING			
	Etoile Violette Large flowers which are violet-purple with a reddish tint ~~when young.~~ £4.85 *Add Petit Faucon here*	£4.00	
	Wyevale This has dark-~~purple~~, *blue* scented flowers that last from August to October. £7.00	~~£6.50~~ £4.25	

Exam Practice 3 Document 4 ctd

WINTER FLOWERING

Wisley Cream This has light-green leaves with greenish-cream flowers. £5.00   £3.50

(Add Cirrhosa balearica here)

Ourika Valley This is a hardy plant that has pale-yellow flowers. £8.25   ~~£6.75~~ £5.99

Freckles As its name suggests, this has heavily-speckled, creamy-pink flowers. Much prettier than the description. £9.00   £7.75

You will find many more varieties in our nursery. However, if you would like a particular species then we can order it for you. Please ask at our Customer Services desk.

Niobe Rich deep-red/flowers from late spring to early autumn. ~~£12.99~~   £10.99

Summer Snow Flowers between midsumma and mid-autumn. The creamy-white flowers are slightly scented. ~~£5.99~~   £4.75

Ascotiensus Bright-blue flowers throughout Summer. ~~£7.99~~   £5.50

Petit Faucon This is excellent value as it flowers for over three months. The flowers are a beautiful deep blue with yellow-orange stamens when young. ~~£12.50~~   £10.50

Cirrhosa balearica The green foliage of this plant turns to bronze during winter. As an added bonus, its creamy pink flowers are fragrant. ~~£9.00~~   £7.50

Exam Practice 3 Reference Sheet

Information on this sheet is not to be copied. It indicates the house style required for the documents.

Document 1

Display the paragraphs and their headings as shown here.

Monday 9.00 am – 11.30 am	**<u>Keyboarding Workshop</u>** This workshop shows you the correct way to keyboard. You will soon be typing fast and accurately. All materials are provided. Lisa Jenkins £56.00
Thursday 2.30 pm – 4.30 pm	**<u>Desktop Publishing Workshop</u>** You will learn how to set out newsletters, invitations and notices. Inserting graphics and drawings are part of this exciting one-day course. Peter Norris £85.00

Document 3

Diagram – This does not have to be reproduced in this exact size and can be adjusted to fit the space available in your document. Either squares or rectangles can be used. Use any font size or style.

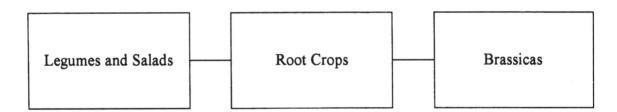

Document 4

Use capitalisation and a four-column layout as in this specimen layout.

SHADY AREAS

	<u>Midnight Magic</u>	£10.99	£8.99
	This fabulous dark-blue flowering plant will thrive in a shady area.		
	<u>Midsummer Dream</u>	£12.50	£9.75
	Creamy-pink and white flowers all summer long from this leafy plant.		

Exam Practice 4 Document 1

Recall this document stored as CRAFT1.
Display it as indicated on the Reference Sheet and
amend it as shown. Save as CRAFT1A and
print one copy.

CRAFT MONTHLY ← Use a larger font and centre

Craft Monthly is a specialist magazine featuring all types of craft work.

The magazine is packed with features including:

step-by-step guides
patterns and scale drawings for craft projects

hints and tips by experts
Where to buy
what to look for.

Please add a full-page border

September
The ~~October~~ issue of Craft Monthly has the first of a 7-part series on ceramics. This special supplement tells you all you need to know to start this fascinating hobby or to improve your existing skills.

The series will look at the history, materials, equipment, tools, glazing, firing and decoration techniques. Some of the best-known experts in this subject will be revealing the secrets of their success.

Insert a text box in the centre, 8cm wide x 2cm high with the words

Monthly
Price £2.95

Centre these words.

Shade this box and use a different font size and style

A chance to win a weekend course at one of the country's leading studios is also on offer.

Next issue on sale 7 September.

Change Craft Monthly to Craft News throughout

Key in using a consistent typeface and layout. Save as CRAFT2 and print on one side of a sheet of A4 paper.

Insert horizontal dividers at places marked ——#——. These may be displayed in any style.

Porcelain

We can all enjoy the beauty of a well-sculpted and painted piece of porcelain. It first appeared in China in the 7th century during the reign of the T'ang dynasty.

Porcelain came to Europe via Palestine during the Crusades and was literally worth its weight in gold.

Many people believed it had magical powers. A common superstition was that if a poisoned drink was poured into porcelain it would shatter the drinking vessel. ——//——

Use a two-column layout for this section

Early, detailed reports of porcelain manufacture were brought to Europe in 1295, and attempts were made to copy it.

However, it took until the end of the 17th century before soft frit porcelain was made in France.

The formula for hard porcelain was discovered in 1709 by Johann Friedrich Böttger in Meissen.

By the end of the 18th century, frit porcelain was manufactured under the name of pâte tendre artificielle, at Sèvres, France.

The formula had been invented in 1673 and manufactured in 1695 by Pierre Chicaneau in his Saint-Cloud factory. ——//——

Bone china, which was invented by an Englishman, Thomas Frye, in 1748 will be the subject of the second article in this fascinating series.

Insert a clip-art picture here

Exam Practice 4 Document 3

Recall this document stored as CRAFT3.   . Insert a
header *Craft News Supplement* in the centre and a footer
Article 1 in a series of 7 at the right margin using an 8
point font for both. Number the pages at the bottom left
starting with page 12. Adjust the line length to 11.5cm
and use full justification. Save as CRAFT3A and
print one copy in double-line spacing except where
indicated.   Use a 10 point font for the text.

Guide to Ceramics Part I

The basic materials used for the manufacture of ceramics are clay and kaolin.
According to composition, use, firing, temperature and deformation in fire,
they can be classified as various types of clay. These are:

brick
earthenware
porous (whiteware)   *Use bullet points for this section*
stoneware
porcelain.

Inset this paragraph 20 mm from both margins

These clays are often used as components of man-made
ceramic bodies. Ceramic working bodies can be either plastic
or non-plastic.

Plastic Materials ◄   *Emphasise this heading*

These are fine-ground rocks formed by clay materials whose particles are less
than 2mm in size. The basic property of these materials is their ability, when
mixed with water, to form a mouldable body. It does not develop cracks when
bent, and retains its shape when dried and fired.

This paragraph in single-line spacing

However, a ceramic body composed only of plastic materials would also have
its drawbacks. These include shrinkage and poor drying. In order to overcome
these problems, Grog and fluxes are added to the basic composition.

Kaolin

Kaolin is a soft, white, earthy material that is dry to the touch.
When mixed with water it becomes fairly plastic and retains its
colour when fired. Kaolin is refractory (fire-resistant). It is usually
produced by kaolinization (weathering) of feldspathic rocks.
Its basic component is the rock kaolinite $A2_2O_3 \cdot 2SiO_2 \cdot 2H_2O$.

Primary Clays

Exam Practice 4 Document 3 ctd

These are a mixture of clay minerals according to the exact composition of the parent rock and its means of decomposition.

Secondary Clays

These are ~~materials~~ Clays that have been transported from the original site of formation. The main agent of transportation is water, ~~however, wind and glacier-borne clays have been known~~.

Fireclays

These withstand very high temperatures of at least 1580°C. Fireclays are normally used for furnace lining and other technical purposes.

Other secondary clays include stoneware, earthenware, brick, Marls and Bentonitic.

Ceramic Batches

Most clays need to be processed before use. Once prepared the ceramic batch should be easy to shape, have low shrinkage and keep its shape when fired. More information on processing will be given later in the series.

Testing ← Emphasise this heading

Testing your ceramic materials before use is essential. This will also be featured fully later on in the series. However, as an example, we will look at the shrinkage test.

First of all make a bar from the ceramic material and mark a precise line, 10cm will be sufficient. See Fig. 1.

Insert diagram from Reference Sheet here

Allow the bar to dry and then measure your line. You can then fire the bar and measure again. The shrinkage rate can be calculated using the following formula:

$$(a - b) \div (a \times 100)$$ where a = original distance and b = distance after firing.

The resulting figure is the percentage of shrinkage. This should not exceed 8–10%.

Exam Practice 4 Document 4

Recall this document stored as CRAFT4, and display as the example on the Reference Sheet. Complete the document. Save as CRAFT4A and print one copy.

CLASSIFIED ADVERTISEMENTS

The advertisements listed below have been booked for the September Ceramic Supplement. The copy and rough drafts have already been sent to the designer ~~for pasting up~~.

COPY	CONTACT NAME	SIZE	PRICE
Exeter Ceramics We can supply all types of clay, glazes, tools and equipment. Competitive prices and free delivery within the Exeter area. (Ceramic Suppliers)	Duncan MacDonald	¼ page	£450
Add John + Joan Hansford here **Vinton Ltd** Suppliers of raw materials for all types of glazes. Trade enquiries only. For full details call 01721 564632. (Glaze Specialists)	Lorraine Swift	⅛ page	£250
Carlton Pottery If you are interested in learning more about this fascinating craft, then try one of our courses. We offer day, evening, weekend and residential courses. Suitable for beginners and improvers. For further information on our wide range of courses, call 0138 2839183. (Specialist Courses)	Peter ~~Ellesmere~~ Richards	Full page	~~£2000~~ £1500
Add George Lewis Studio here **Children's Pottery** Our pottery workshops are very popular with children aged 8 to 14. Classes are limited to 5 children and cost £45 for a 3-hour session. All materials are provided although children will need to bring protective clothing. Courses held each day during the school holidays. To book a place telephone 01813 2837162. (Bath area). (General Courses)	Margaret Seymour	~~Full~~ ¼ page	£450 ~~£1800~~

Add The Potter's Wheel™ here

John and Joan Hawsford   Joan Hawsford   1/3 page   £675

For all your ceramic needs.
We stock the largest range of
materials at the lowest prices.
Delivery guaranteed within 4
days of order. (Ceramic
Supplies).

George Lewis Studio   George Lewis   Full page   £2000

For courses on decoration techniques
visit my studio in Taunton. Our
specially-designed workshops are
suitable for beginners to advanced
students. All materials are included
in workshop fees. One-day
courses start at £85. Contact
George Lewis on 01239 4242771
for details of our winter courses.
(Specialist courses)

The Potter's Wheel™   Mick Bennett   1/2 page   £900

Suppliers of quality equipment to
trade and general public. Personal
callers to our warehouse are welcome.
Opening hours 10am - 5pm Monday
to Saturday. Alternatively, browse
through our fully-illustrated catalogue
and price list. Our prices are always
competitive. The Potter's Wheel™ Studio,
Brick Lane, Lowestoft. Telephone Mick
Bennett on 01282 242628 for further
information. (Ceramic Supplies)

Exam Practice 4 Reference Sheet

Information on this sheet is not to be copied. It indicates the house style required for the documents.

Document 1

Display the paragraphs as shown here.

Each month this exciting new magazine will feature a needlework technique. Cross-stitch, embroidery, and smocking are just a few that will be featuring in the coming months.

Patterns and step-by-step instructions will be featured from leading designers, together with articles on how to frame your work professionally.

Document 3

Diagram – This does not have to be reproduced in this exact size and can be adjusted to fit the space available in your document. Either squares or rectangles can be used. Use any font size or style.

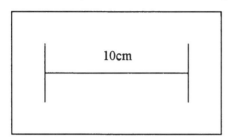
10cm

Fig. 1

Document 4

Use capitalisation and a five-column layout as in this specimen layout.

COPY	CONTACT NAME	SIZE	PRICE	TYPE
BATH CRAFTS We stock all your craft needs: aids, threads, scissors, backing material, wadding, etc all at low prices. Call 012256 382828 for a free catalogue.	Megan Tyler	¼ page	£300	General Stockists
EMBROIDERY WORKSHOPS One-day workshops in various embroidery techniques. Courses suitable for beginners, intermediate and advanced students. Call Rachael Webb today for details.	Rachael Webb	½ page	£650	Specialist Courses

Recall this document stored as CRUISE1
Display it as indicated on the Reference Sheet and
amend it as shown. Save as CRUISE1A and
print one copy.

2

H_2O Cruises™ ← Centre this heading

In association with

The Preferred Travel Company
Bath Branch

Invite you to a cruise evening ← Shade this box and use a different font style and size
on

21 May ← Use a larger font size

at

The Preferred Travel Company, High Street, Bath

8.00 pm
Video presentation – see some of the fabulous cruises for yourself.
The video shows each of the company's major ships.

8.30 pm
Add a full-page border
Refreshments

9.00 pm
An opportunity to ask questions and book the cruise of a lifetime.

This is an exciting opportunity to find out more about the H_2O Cruises™ wonderful holidays. Mr David Krüger Managing Director will be on hand to answer any of your questions

Special deals available for customers who book a holiday at the event.

Insert a text box here 10 cm wide x 2cm high
with the words

Win a luxury cruise
Free draw for a 7-night Italian Cruise
Centre the text box and the words.

Exam Practice 5 Document 2

Key in using a consistent typeface and layout. Save as CRUISE 2 and print on one side of a sheet of A4 paper.

Report on Trading – H₂O Cruises™ ← *Emphasise this heading*

Add a clip-art picture here

The H₂O Cruises™ division of the corporation has had an excellent trading year. The increase in passenger numbers exceeded target and the majority of cruises were booked to capacity.

The increased number of bookings meant that turnover has gone up by 35%. Enquiries for cruise holidays also increased dramatically.

This has been estimated to be over 45%.

Insert horizontal dividers at places marked →✗

Over 10,000 customers received a questionnaire after they had completed their holiday. The response rate was high with 52% of customers responding.

From these replies we have been able to analyse our customers' needs and it is hoped that we will be able to act upon their suggestions in the coming year.

Some of the more important points are given below.

—————————✗—————————

Use a two-column layout for that section

Many customers felt that the service given by our crew was excellent. However, ¹/₃ felt that improvements could be made with regard to the slow service at meal times.

Cleanliness of some areas of the ship(s) was also an issue, in particular on the Fiesta. Of the 1600 replies from Fiesta clients, over ¼ felt that the decks and walkways were not cleaned to a satisfactory standard.

This has been investigated and it is anticipated that this issue has been resolved.

—————————✗—————————

The current market share held by H₂O Cruises™ has been calculated to be 29%. This was calculated using the following formula. Obviously all figures are estimates.

$$N = tm \text{ (total market)} \div np \text{ (number of passengers on } H_2O \text{ Cruises}^{TM}) \times 100 \simeq 29\%$$

Recall this document stored as CRUISE3. Insert a header Information Sheet in the centre and a footer Ref 1²346A at the left-hand margin, using a point 14 font for both. Number the pages at the top left starting with page 7. Adjust the line length to 12 cm + use full justification. Save as CRUISE3A and print one copy using treble-line spacing except where indicated.

CRUISING HOLIDAYS

Taking a cruise may seem to many of us to be beyond our budget. However, this is not the case. A cruise can be as affordable as any package holiday.

British holidaymakers are beginning to ~~realise the enjoyment~~ appreciate the fun that can be had on a cruise. Approximately 650,000 British people took a cruise holiday in 1997 compared with 298,000 in 1993. However, as around 17 million British people booked a package holiday in 1997, it can be seen that cruises have room to improve their market share.

Cost

The price of a 7-~~day~~ night cruise can cost as little as £500 per person. When you take into account that all meals, entertainment and children's facilities are included in this price, this can compare favourably with other types of holiday.

Entertainment

Inset this paragraph 30 mm from both margins

These days most cruises offer plenty of opportunity to visit new places by having a well-planned itinerary. For the few days you are confined on board the liner there are plenty of activities on offer. You can take your pick from gymnasiums, theatres, cinemas, ~~health and beauty treatments~~, deck sports, lectures and swimming.

As some of the larger ships have over 2,000 passengers it is unlikely you will become bored. There will always be someone who is willing to have a drink or exchange stories with you.

Activity Cruises

If you enjoy an active holiday or like to learn new skills, then why not combine these with a cruise? There are many different cruises available which combine both. The activities on offer include creative writing, painting, health and beauty, ~~rock and roll~~ – something to suit all tastes.

This paragraph only in single-line spacing

Exam Practice 5 Document 3 ctd

Destinations

tour operators

You can take a cruise to almost anywhere. Many ~~companies~~ offer a two-part holiday. This gives you the opportunity to spend half your holiday at sea and the rest at a hotel.

night

The length of the cruise varies enormously from a three-~~day~~ break to a worldwide cruise lasting several months.

Popular ~~cruise~~ destinations include Jamaica, Barbados, the Greek Islands and even Florida.

Accommodation

There is a wide choice of accommodation on board most liners. This generally ranges from a small cabin with private bathroom to large suites, which include a sitting room, bedroom and bathroom. Outside cabins – those which are facing the sea – cost more than inside cabins. ~~Inside cabins do not have a sea view.~~

It is possible to book a 4-berth cabin, these are great for families with young children.
Given below is a typical cabin layout. *Insert the Diagram from the Reference Sheet here.*

Food and Drink

You will certainly eat well on your holiday. Many tours offer 6 meals each day – some even offer 8.

A typical day's meals would include:

Apply bullet points to this section

full breakfast
elevenses
three-course buffet lunch/
afternoon tea
four-course evening meal
midnight buffet.

Change liner to Ship throughout this document.

Recall this document stored under CRUISE4 and display as the example on the Reference Sheet. Complete the document, save as CRUISE4A, and print one copy.

H₂O Cruises™

June Vacations

Given below are just a few of the cruises we offer. These vacations all have a start date in June. For further information contact Elizabeth Chaine on 01727 4422176.

SHIP	DETAILS	PRICE PER PERSON FROM
St Lucia	Fly to Orlando and meet your ship at Fort Lauderdale. The ship docks at Nassau, San Juan, St John and St Thomas, Half Moon Cay returning to Fort Lauderdale. Return flight from Orlando. 7 nights	£750
Fiesta	This cruise offers a variety of ~~cities~~ towns, islands and beaches to ensure you enjoy the best of the Carribean. You can enjoy shopping in some of the great cities followed by exploring unspoilt islands. 14 ~~10~~ nights Add Fiesta info here	~~£1450~~ £1675
President	Our Italian cruise is excellent value for money. It is a 7-night cruise but can be extended with a 7-night stay on land.	£720 or
	Fly to Palma to join the President. The ship calls at Rome, Naples, Messina (Sicily), Malta and Sardinia. You then return to Palma for your flight home or to transfer to your chosen accommodation. 7 or 14 nights	£1300
Maria	Our second Caribbean cruise has a different route but is equally exciting. This cruise can be combined with a 7-night stay on land. (Add Maria info here)	650 ~~£595~~ or £1100

We can offer some excellent discounts on any of the above vacations. Children aged 12 or under travel at ½ price.

If you are celebrating a special occasion while on one of our cruises please tell us. We can arrange for champagne, chocolates and flowers to be delivered to your cabin.

Fiesta Information

Fly to Montego Bay to meet the Fiesta for an action-packed voyage. Ports of call include Santa Domingo, British Virgin Island Tortola, Antigua, Dominica, St Lucia, Grenada, Barbados, St Vincent, Guadeloupe, St Kitts, Serena Cay. The Fiesta then returns to Montego Bay for your flight back to the UK. 15 nights

Maria Information

Your holiday starts when you land in Barbados. First call is St Lucia, followed by Grenada, Margarita, Curaçao and Aruba. Return to Barbados for a further one-week stay or flight home.
7 or 14 nights.

Exam Practice 5 Reference Sheet

Information on this sheet is not to be copied. It indicates the house style required for the documents.

Document 1

Display the paragraphs and their headings as shown here.

7.30 pm	Introduction to the company. A chance to have a glass of wine and look at some of our fabulous brochures.
7.45 pm	A welcome address from our Managing Director.

Document 3

Diagram – This does not have to be reproduced in this exact size and can be adjusted to fit the space available in your document. Either squares or rectangles can be used. Use any font size or style.

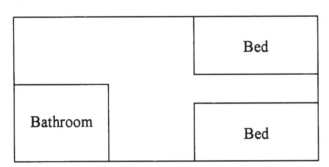

Typical cabin layout

Document 4

Use capitalisation and a four-column layout as in this specimen layout.

SHIP	DETAILS	PRICE PER PERSON	NUMBER OF NIGHTS
CHARLOTTE	Fly to Orlando and meet your ship at Fort Lauderdale. Ports of call include Playa del Carmen, Cozumel, Grand Cayman, Ocho Rios, Half Moon Cay before returning to Fort Lauderdale. Fly home after a relaxing night in a hotel in Orlando.	£1350	14
ROSEANNE	Fly to Cyprus and transfer to your ship at Limassol. Ports of call are Volos, Mytilene, Istanbul, Kusadasi, Kos before returning to Limassol. Fly home from Cyprus.	£850	7

Exam Practice 6 Document 1

Recall this document stored as LIFE1. Display it as indicated on the Reference sheet and around it as shown. Save as LIFE1A and print one copy.

LIFE STYLE MAGAZINE ← *Shade this box and use a larger font*

The third edition *of our quarterly magazine*

Insert a text box. 8cm wide x 4cm high with the words
SUMMER SPECIAL
HEALTH AND BEAUTY ISSUE
Centre the text box on the page and the words within it.

All you need to know – the latest ideas and articles on

Keeping Fit
Sports, equipment, exercise. *The latest in sports crazes. Where to find the equipment, where to go.*
Looking Good ·
The latest in fashion, make-up, hair and style.

Feeling Great
Healthy recipes, *together with the latest health up-dates.*

Features on: *Add a full-page border*

hay fever
stress
~~dieting~~ *healthy eating*
the most fashionable places to holiday
the latest activity holidays

Price £2.75
Order a copy from your newsagent now! ← *Use a different font size and style*

Everything you need to keep you looking good and feeling great *throughout the Summer.*

Make-up advice for a natural-looking summer *from the professional make-up artists.*

Having a bad hair day? We test the most fashionable hair salons.

Key in using a consistent typeface and layout. Save as LIFE2 and print on one side of a sheet of A4 paper.

Hay Fever

Emphasise all headings

If you are one of Britain's 3 million hay fever ~~suffers~~ sufferers, you will appreciate how this can ruin your summer, making you a virtual prisoner indoors.

The number of ~~suffers~~ sufferers of this summer complaint has doubled over the past 10 years.

What is it?

Hay fever is an allergic response to pollen. This can be from trees, grasses and flowers.

The allergic reaction occurs when the immune system treats the pollen particles as allergens – invaders.

Add horizontal dividers at places marked ——//

What are the symptoms?

Common symptoms include:

itchy or weeping eyes
rhinitis (inflammation of the nasal passages)
sneezing.

Apply bullet points to this section

These are caused by the body responding to the allergens.

Can it be treated?

```
The good news is that hay fever can be treated
successfully.
```

There are a number of treatments on the market that you can buy over the counter at your local pharmacist. However, if your symptoms persist it is always worth visiting your GP.

————————//————————

Use a two-column layout for this section

Conventional Medicine

The most common treatment is by antihistamines, which will help reduce weeping eyes and nose. However, you may need a decongestant as well.

Although antihistamine is a powerful remedy, many of the medicines can also cause side effects. These may include drowsiness and insomnia.

Alternative Treatment

There are many alternative treatments that claim to alleviate the symptoms of hay fever. Some of the most common are homeopathy and acupuncture.

————————//————————

Add a clip-art picture here

Exam Practice 6 Document 3

Recall this document stored as LIFE3. . Insert a header LIFESTYLE at the left-hand margin and a footer Special Issue at the right-hand margin using a 10point font for both. Number the pages starting with page 22. Adjust the line length to 12cm and use full justification and a size 12 font. Print one copy in double-line spacing. SAVE AS LIFE3A.

Healthy Eating ← Emphasise and centre this heading

In the past the most usual way to calculate if you were overweight was to use a weight table. However, this is not the most accurate method, as it does not take into account various other factors such as your build ~~or frame~~.

The recommended way to calculate your body weight is the Body Mass Index (BMI). It is calculated by dividing the weight in kilograms by the square of the height in metres.

To do this, weigh yourself in kilograms and measure your height in metres. Divide your weight by your height in m^2. For example, for a person who weighs 65 kg and has a height of 1.6m the calculation would be:

$$65 \div 1.6^2 (1.6 \times 1.6) = 65 \div 2.56 = 25.4$$

The final figure is your BMI and you compare it to the following:

BMI 20 or below – Underweight
BMI 20 – 24.9 – Normal
BMI 25 – 29.9 – Plump
BMI 30 – 39.9 – Moderately overweight
BMI 40 and above – Very overweight

← Apply bullet points to this section

This paragraph in single-line spacing

If your calculation tells you that you have a BMI of 25 or over then you may wish to lose some weight. It is very important that you consult your GP before entering into any type of diet.

decide
If you do ~~have~~ to lose some weight then adopt a sensible eating plan. You ~~must~~ Should include plenty of fresh vegetables and salads, together with protein and fibre-giving foods such as meat, bread, fish, cheese, etc. Try to cut down on the Sugar- or fat-loaded foods such as sweets, Chocolate, Crisps, fizzy drinks and alcohol. Your GP will be able to advise you on a sensible, healthy eating plan.

Exam Practice 6 Document 3 ctd

Vitamins and Minerals

It is important that you have a diet rich in vitamins and minerals. These help your body stay fit and healthy. Green vegetables are a good source of vitamins B_2 and C.

Cereals are also a good source of the B vitamins such as B_{12} and B_6. They also contain minerals such as iron and folic acid. For example, a 30g serving of Cereal with 125ml of semi-skimmed milk can provide 75μ of iron, that is 75% of the recommended daily allowance (RDI).

Carbohydrates

The main carbohydrates are glucose ($C_6H_{12}O_6$), fructose (found in fruit) starch, sugar and cellulose (found in plants).

Insert this paragraph 25mm from both margins

These are essential energy-giving foods. Although most carbohydrates are good for us, foods high in sugar should be eaten in moderation.

Fats

These are also energy-giving foods but, because of their high cholesterol and calorie values, should be eaten in moderation. These foods include butter, margarine, cooking oil, some processed foods such as crisps and foods that have been fried.

Proteins

Milk, eggs, cheese, fish, pulses and nuts all contain proteins. These are body-building foods that assist growth and repair damaged tissue. Muscles, skin, hair and nails are all nearly 100% protein.

Place diagram from reference sheet here

To maintain a healthy diet it is recommended that you eat the following portions daily.

Recall the document stored as LIFE4 and display as the example on the reference sheet. Complete the document and print one copy. Save as LIFE4A

The Most Fashionable Hairdressers

Our intrepid reporter ~~Frances~~ *Françoise* Page was sent to investigate some of the most fashionable hairdressers. / As she feels her hair is already perfect she asked four testers to have various treatments. Here are the results. The star rating is 5 = excellent, 1 = poor.

EUGÈNE
LONDON

The tester, Louise decided to ~~go for~~ *have* a complete restyle of her shoulder-length blonde hair. Clutching a photo of an unsuitable style she ventured in.

****

JOHN AND JANE
MANCHESTER

Kathy was our tester in Manchester. She decided to have a restyle and blonde highlights put through her rather mousy-coloured hair. Kathy mentioned this when booking the appointment and was asked to have a consultation prior to the appointment / *being booked*.

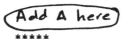

*****

GREENS
~~LEEDS~~
YORK

Roberta booked an appointment for her long hair to be styled for a special night out. She explained to the stylist how she wanted her hair to look and sat back to relax. One hour later she emerged feeling happy with the result but extremely unhappy with the price of £55.   * ~~**~~

HEAD MASTERS
BRISTOL

Suzy tested this fairly new hairdressers. Suzy already has a perm and colour on her hair but decided to try highlights as well. She booked an appointment with ~~Peter~~, a senior stylist.   *David*

When Suzy complained, she was treated in an off-hand manner and the manager would not reduce the fee of £65.

*

Change hairdressers to Salons throughout

(*) Eugène's Senior stylist had a 15-minute Consultation with Louise. She gently but firmly told Louise that her suggested style would not suit her and gave several alternatives. Louise was thrilled with her new hair style and the service she received.

(△) The stylist and colourist both talked through the various options and a style, colour and appointment/were agreed upon. Result? Kathy looks fabulous and feels it was well worth the expense.

(□) David did not comment upon the condition of Suzy's hair or ask questions about her previous treatments. The result is that her hair is now dry + split and the highlights cannot be seen.

Exam Practice 6 Reference Sheet

Information on this sheet is not to be copied. It indicates the house style required for the documents.

Document 1

Display the paragraphs and their headings as shown here.

<u>Keeping Fit</u>   The latest fitness news. Some of the most fashionable sports around at the moment. Who takes part in what? Our guide to the celebrities keeping fit.

<u>Looking Good</u>   The Paris fashion shows had some unexpected stars. Who were they and when will we see them again? We have the answers.

Document 3

Diagram – This does not have to be reproduced in this exact size and can be adjusted to fit the space available in your document. Either circles or ovals can be used. Use any font size or style.

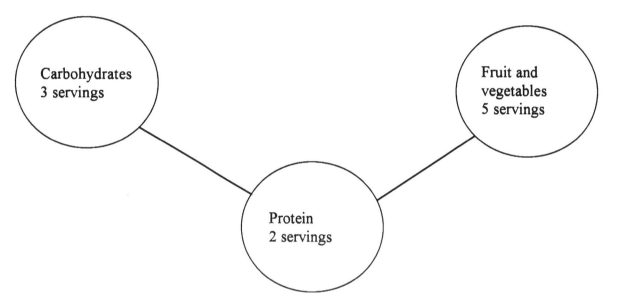

Document 4

Use capitalisation and a three-column layout as in this specimen layout.

		Star Rating
HEAD START Bath	Maggie decided to have her long, dark-brown hair cut short. She talked this through with the Senior Stylist, Alan who made some sensible suggestions. After some deliberation, she decided to keep her hair at shoulder-length. However, the cut and blow-dry was excellent.	****

Exam Practice 7 Document 1

Recall this document stored as FRANCH1 and display as the example on the Reference sheet.
Save as FRANCH1A and print one copy

Are you fed up with working for someone else?

Would you like to be your own boss?

Use a shaded box and a larger font

Find out more at the

BUSINESSPLUS® EXHIBITION

This year's Businessplus® Exhibition offers you the opportunity to find out how to become your own boss and run a successful business.

Franchising is the modern way to start a business as many of the usual risks have been eliminated.

Your initial investment may be as little as £5,000. *Use a different type size and style*

We will be offering the following workshops for those interested in ~~franching.~~ franchising.

Add a full-page border

Saturday
11.00 am

Service Industry

There are a number of service industry opportunities. These range from estate management to financial advice. Investment can be as little as £8,500

Saturday
2.00 am

Commercial Cleaning

This is a major growth area in franchising. Start-up costs can be as little as £2,000.

Insert a text box measuring 2 cm high x 11 cm wide, in the centre of the page. Insert the words For further details on the Exhibition, Contact Stan Davies on 01827 3388119 Centre these words within the box

Key in using a consistent typeface and layout. Save as FRANCH2 and print on one side of a sheet of A4 paper.

Franchising ← *Emphasise ALL headings*

All franchises work in the same way – that is, the franchisee pays to use the business services, goods and name provided by the franchisor.

However, there are a number of different types of franchise.

These include:

//

Investment

These require a substantial amount of capital to be invested by the franchisee.

Usually the franchisee will employ staff, including managerial, to run the business on a day-to-day basis. Often large food or hotel chains are run in this way.

Insert horizontal dividers at places marked —//—.

Executive

These are generally the white-collar business services, including financial services, consultancy and personnel. These are often managed by just one person. However, it is best to have had previous experience in the chosen field.

Retail

Retail franchises often require a high level of capital investment. This is because premises, shop fittings and stock all need to be purchased.

The benefit of a retail franchise is that the business can usually be sold as a going concern should the owner wish to retire or capitalise on his or her investment. The franchisee generally takes an active role in the business.

Use a two-column layout for this section

//

Add a clip-art picture here

There are also other types of franchise such as sales and distribution that can be set up with relatively little capital.

Recall this document stored as FRANCH3. Insert a header Business Information Sheet 164039 at the left-hand margin and a footer Author R. Mañoso at the right-hand margin. Use a point 10 font for both. Number the pages at the bottom centre starting with page 2. Adjust the line length to 12.5 cm and use full justification. Print one copy in double-line spacing. SAVE as FRANCH3A.

Business Franchising ← *Centre and emphasise this heading*

What is Franchising?

Inset this section 30 mm from both margins

Franchising in its most basic form is an arrangement between one party, ~~the franchisor,~~ who has a blueprint and system for a business, and a second party who wishes to copy the business.

The franchisor – the person or company with the idea and system – should have developed a tested blueprint for a successful business. They will have ~~tested~~ *investigated* the market, developed the product or service and attained the skills necessary to make the business a success.

The franchisee – the person who wishes to copy the business – should receive training to run their business and be offered help and advice from the franchisor when necessary.

What are the Benefits of Franchising?

As previously mentioned, the franchisee should be given full training in the business and be able to ask for help when needed.

This means it is an ideal way to start running your own business as you should be supported by a group of people who have already assessed the market.

Some franchisors offer their franchisees an exclusive ~~area~~ *territory* so that competition is limited. It is of course in the franchisor's interests to have successful franchisees.

What do I Need to Start my own Business?

In order to make a success of your business you will need the following:

Capital. As well as your initial investment you will also need money to live on while you are setting up your business.

Apply bullet points to these ~~three~~ items

Exam Practice 7 Document 3 ctd

Time and effort. Running your own business takes a great deal of time and effort, especially when you first start. If you wish to work nine to five, five days a week, then maybe you are not suited to running a business.

Experience. Many franchisees have not had previous experience in running a business in their market area. *However, in order to maximise your chances of success, try to find a business that you should capitalises on your existing skills.*

This paragraph in subjective spacing

What are the Drawbacks of Franchising?

Commitment

You must put in a great deal of time and ~~effort~~ on building up your business. This means long hours, often unsociable. This can often put a strain on family life, so you will need support and often practical help from your friends and family.

As the franchisor may take a percentage of your turnover, you will need to generate a larger turnover in order to provide an income *sufficient for your needs.*

For example, if the franchise agreement states that you must pay, say 3% of your turnover in fees, you will need to increase turnover by approximately 5% in order to achieve the same level of success as a non-franchised business.

Copy diagram from reference sheet here

Exam Practice 7 Document 4

> Recall this document stored as FRANCH4, and display as the example on the reference sheet. Complete the document and print one copy. Save as FRANCH4A.

Minutes of Meeting of the Exhibition Committee

Held on 21 October
at 3.00pm
at Businessplan© Head office

Present: Carrie Lyon, Laurence Brady, Hamish Grant, Déborah Raul

Apologies: Michael Read, Paul Douglas (late arrival)

1 MINUTES OF LAST MEETING	These were agreed and signed.
2 MATTERS ARISING	Booking of conference centre. DR confirmed that the conference centre has accepted our booking and that all services requested can be provided.

(Add Item 3 here)

4 ADVERTISING 4.1 Trade Stands	This was ~~talked about~~ discussed at some length. Invitations to book stands will be sent to all regular exhibitors. New franchisees will also be invited. These must go out within the next few weeks in order to maximise bookings. Overseas companies should be ~~faxed~~ contacted before the end of the month.
	Once CL has calculated the break-even point the intensity of the advertising can be discussed. (Action CL)
4.2 Visitors	This will be delayed until the required no. of bookings have been made. (Paul Douglas arrived at 3.20pm)
5 PRINTING	The printing of information packs for traders can now be confirmed. It is anticipated that approx. ~~800~~ 1000 will be required. After some discussion, it was agreed the contract for printing should be given to Marshall & Co. LB to make the final arrangements. (Action ~~LB~~ ~~DR~~)

Change conference to exhibition throughout this document

6 SECURITY	The conference centre confirmed that they can provide all necessary security personnel if required. This is at a cost of ~~£1800~~ £1600 per day. DR to consider alternative arrangements. (Action DR)
7 ANY OTHER BUSINESS	There were no other matters arising.
8 DATE OF NEXT MEETING	This will be held on ~~20~~ 21 December in the conference room at ~~2.30~~ 3.00 pm
	The meeting closed at 5.00 pm.

Item 3   COSTINGS

CL reported that, having ~~confirmation~~ received of costs from the Conference Centre, it is now possible to calculate the charges to both exhibitors and visitors. This is calculated as follows:

$$C + o \div e = n$$

(Conference Centre charges + other overheads ÷ number of exhibitors = break even point)

From this it should be possible to ensure a profit of approximately 25% after the visitor(s) entrance fees have been added. CL to give a detailed breakdown to all concerned as soon as possible. (Action CL)

Exam Practice 7 Reference Sheet

Information on this sheet is not to be copied. It indicates the house style required for the documents.

Document 1

Display the paragraphs and their headings as shown here.

Saturday 9.00 am   <u>Retail Industry</u>

                          There are many retail opportunities from some of the country's best-known High-Street chains.

Sunday 10.00 am   <u>Management</u>

                          If you have proven skills and experience in management there are a wide number of franchises suitable for you.

Document 3

Diagram – This does not have to be reproduced in this exact size and can be adjusted to fit the space available in your document. Either squares or rectangles can be used. Use any font size or style.

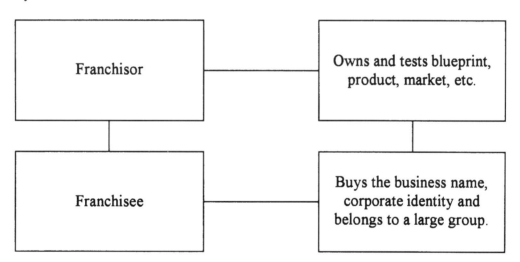

Document 4

Use capitalisation and a four-column layout as in this specimen layout.

			Action
5 <u>Equipment</u>	HG stated that new equipment and stands would need to be purchased this year. HG agreed to investigate costs and report back.		HG
6 <u>Catering</u>	PD agreed to investigate local catering companies to ascertain costs and level of service provided.		PD

Exam Practice 8 Document 1

Recall this document stored as DECOR1. Display it as indicated on the Reference Sheet and amend as shown. Save as DECOR1A and print one copy.

Life Style Magazine ← *Shade this box and use a larger font size.*

AGENDA AND NOTES FOR CHAIR

1 APOLOGIES *Add a full-page border*

2 MINUTES OF PREVIOUS MEETING

3 MATTERS ARISING Check that Lorraine ~~Dyer~~ Hughes has confirmed the booking of a house at St Ives for the Christmas ~~on the Beach~~ by the Sea feature.

4 ~~JULY~~ NOVEMBER ISSUE CAR BOOT BARGAINS
Simon ~~Kevill~~ *to report on progress. Check that Simon has contacted a celebrity interior designer and a stylist for the photographic shoot next month.*

5 PLANNING — JAN TO MARCH ISSUES
Feature reports to be given by Simon, Lorraine and Melanie. The list of proposed features will be circulated within the next few days. Advance material to be prepared within three weeks.

6 ANY OTHER BUSINESS

~~8~~ 7 DATE OF NEXT MEETING
Suggest 22 of next month at 10.00am in the Conference Room.

Insert a text box 3 cm high × 8 cm wide and centre on page. Use a different font size and style and centre the words:

Home Features Team Meeting to be held on 18 August at 2.30pm in the Conference Room

> Key in using a consistent typeface and layout. Save as DECOR2 and print on one side of a sheet of A4 paper.

INTERIOR DECORATION

If you wish to brighten up your home but do not have too much money to spend, why not try a paint technique on your walls. Paint techniques such as colourwashing, stencilling, stippling and sponging are all relatively easy to do and cost little. You will however, need a steady hand, time and patience.

(Add clip-art picture here)

(Use a two-column layout for this section)

Before you start, make sure that you prepare your walls properly. If you are not going to remove any existing wallpaper, you will have to wash the walls thoroughly.

Use a solution of sugar soap and water. This is to remove any greasy marks that may affect the paint adhering to the paper.

Should you decide to remove the existing wallpaper, ensure you remove all traces, especially around light switches and skirting boards. You may need to remove or repair any missing or loose patches of plaster.

There are a number of good DIY books specialising in paint techniques on the market, or you can ask at your local DIY store for advice. Follow any instructions carefully and always allow paint to dry thoroughly before applying a second or subsequent coat.

You can experiment with the various paint techniques until you find one that is right for your home.

> Add horizontal dividers at places marked
> —+—

Exam Practice 8 Document 3

Recall this draft stored as DECOR3. Insert a header Interior Design – Materials at the left-hand margin, and a footer ©Laura Morris January 1998 at the left-hand margin, using a 10 point font for both. Number the pages at the top right-hand margin starting with page 11. Adjust the line length to 11cm and use full justification and a size 12 font. Save as DECOR3A and print one copy in treble linespacing except where indicated.

HOME DECORATION *(Emphasise all sub-headings)*

Calculating the Materials Required

planning

If you are ~~going~~ to decorate a room you will need to work out the amount of materials required.

Inset this paragraph 20mm from both margins

It is important that you purchase the correct amount before you start work as the shades of paint ~~and wallpapers~~ may vary slightly from batch to batch. Different types of paint such as emulsion or gloss will cover different areas depending on its consistency. Your local Do-It-Yourself store will be able to give advice on this.

Paint

~~As stated above, paint shades can vary from batch to batch, so it is important to purchase the necessary quantity before starting to paint.~~ As a general rule a standard ~~tin~~ can will contain one litre of paint. To decide how much paint to buy, calculate the area to be painted by multiplying the height by the width of each wall and then add all the totals together.

For example, for a room/ with two walls measuring 9ft high x 12ft wide and two walls measuring 9ft high x 10ft wide, the calculation will be $(9 \times 12) \times 2 + (9 \times 10) \times 2$. This will give an answer of 396 ft^2.

To calculate the paint needed for moulded window or door frames, multiply the height by the width of the frames and consider it as a solid surface. For example, for a window measuring 4ft high x 3ft wide, the calculation will be $4 \times 3 = 12$ ft^2.

To paint a moulded door, multiply the height of the door by the width and add one quarter to allow for the increased surface area caused by the moulding. (h x w = a $(a \div 4 = b) + b = c$). For example, for a door measuring 6ft high x 3ft wide, the calculation will be $6 \times 3 = 18$ ft^2, divided by 4 = 4½ ft^2. Now add the original total of 18 ft^2 to ¼ (4½ ft) and the answer will be 22½ ft^2.

Exam Practice 8 Document 3 ctd

Insert here the diagram shown on the reference sheet

Types of Paint

This paragraph only in single-line spacing

There are many different types of paint available, and most have a specific use, for example, paints for wood, walls, pipes, ~~timber~~ and guttering. <u>You will need to find out the type of paint most suitable for the surface you are covering.</u>

The amount of paint you buy will depend on many factors. For example, you will need to buy more paint if any of the following apply:

the type of paint being used is particularly porous
~~if~~ the area being covered is textured
~~if~~ you are painting over a dark colour

Apply bullet points

Once you have calculated the room measurements you should be able to obtain advice from your local Do-It-Yourself store on how much paint will be required, bearing in mind the factors given above.

As well as these factors, keep in mind that different types of paint will cover different amounts of surface area. *For example, a one litre can of emulsion or non-drip gloss paint will cover an area of $12 m^2$ or $130 ft^2$.*

Change Do-It-Yourself to DIY throughout this document.

Exam Practice 8 Document 4

Recall this document stored as DECOR4, and display as the example on the reference sheet. Complete the document and print one copy. Store as DECOR4A.

COLOUR SCHEMES

It can be difficult choosing a colour scheme that is right for your home. *The following list gives some suggestions together with our favourite ranges available at the moment.*

<u>Bedroom</u>

COOL BLUE   Try a cool blue bedroom using ~~bluebell~~ *Cornflower blue* paint for walls with a crisp white for doors, skirtings and ceilings. The Country Flowers range by Hilton-Smith Designs contains a variety of bedlinen, wallpapers and curtains that would complement this colour scheme. Hilton-Smith 0121 2882919

Add Ⓧ here

<u>Living Room</u>

Add Ⓐ here

MELLOW
YELLOW   Pale lemon gives a warm and light feel to any room. In fact *using paint* lemon can make a room seem lighter than white. It is a good contrast to many other colours. The best range of lemon and yellow paints can be found at Pierre Pelletier. Pierre Pelletier ~~0927 451308~~
                0932 451309

<u>Kitchen</u>

Café   *Add ▢ here*
~~COFFEE~~
EXPRESSO *kitchen* appliances are now available with a steel finish, or you can achieve the effect with smaller electrical appliances such as toasters and kettles. This look needs a minimalist approach, so if you like lots of clutter then it may not be right for ~~your home.~~ The Lotus chain has the best range of steel accessories on the market. Lotus 0139 493987

For a fashionable, stylish look try lots of stainless steel. Many *large*

CLASSIC LINES Use any of the neutral colours and shades such as beige, cream or ivory for a cool, classic feel. Complement with neutral cushions and curtains made from natural fibres such as linen or raw silk. The Elegant range from Stylish Homes contains a wide range of curtains and cushions in linen, cotton and muslin. Available from all branches of Russells. 0583 563207

COUNTRY COTTAGE If you like the idea of a country cottage you can easily recreate this in your home by the use of accessories. Bunches of dried herbs and copper saucepans will help you acheive the look. The Farmhouse range of kitchen accessories is excellent. Available at most branches of Sébastien Havamée. 01827 634501

ARABIAN NIGHTS For a dramatic and striking bedroom use strong colours and luxurious fabrics. Silks and satins will bring instant glamour to your bedroom. Try the Midnight Magic range from Charlotte Evans for brilliant jewel-colour bedspreads, cushions and fabrics. Charlotte Evans 0382 192893

2

Exam Practice 8 Reference Sheet

Information on this sheet is not to be copied. It indicates the house style required for the documents.

Document 1

Display the paragraphs and their headings as shown here.

1   <u>Apologies</u>

      Apologies were received from Simon Kevill and Lorraine Hughes.

2   <u>Minutes of Previous Meeting</u>

      A mistake was made in Item 3 Matters Arising. Lorraine Hughes confirmed that the flat had been booked for the High-Rise Edition. This was altered and the Minutes were agreed.

Document 3

Diagram – This does not have to be reproduced in this exact size and can be adjusted to fit the space available in your document. Either squares or rectangles can be used. Use any font size or style.

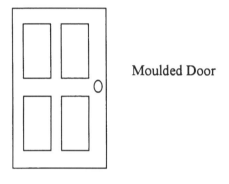 Moulded Door

Document 4

Use capitalisation and a four-column layout as in this specimen layout.

CONTACT

BEDROOM

<u>Nursery Rhymes</u>	For a small child's bedroom you cannot beat the Nursery Range from Weatherall. Their range contains borders, bedlinen, cushions, wallpaper and other accessories in a charming nursery rhyme theme.	Weatheralls 01823 210492

LIVING ROOM

<u>Bright and Bold</u>	For a bright and bold living room, try the latest dramatic colours from Lovells. The paint comes in lime green, brilliant yellow and deep purple. Not for the faint hearted.	Lovells 09235 517624

Proof Reading Exercise 1

First Impressions

You have decided to build your own home. The plans have been drawn up and the specification put together Before you sit back and relax, consider the driveway to your front door.

Remember thaat the driveway is the frist area of your home so ensure it compliments the type of home you have build and the materials you have used. There is a wide variety of materials available, for example, blocks, Bricks, tarmac, shingle and crazy paving.

Before you decide on a design, consider the following:

- the gradient of the land
- the aspect
- the access and egress to the highway and line across the footpath
  the surface water and drainage
- the line of the drive
- the trafffic flow in the road

Errors

1 The full stop is missing.

2 The word **that** has been typed incorrectly.

3 The word **first** contains a typographical error.

4 The word **compliments** has been used instead of **complements**.

5 The word **build** has been typed instead of **built**.

6 The word **variety** contains a typographical error.

7 The word **bricks** has a capital letter.

8 The word **aspect** contains a typographical error.

9 The line beginning **the surface** ... does not have a bullet point.

10 The word **traffic** has been typed incorrectly.

Proof Reading Exercise 2

SUNBURN

The number of cases of skin cancer in the UK has risin sharply in the passed few year.   It is essential that you take care ofyour skin when in the sun.

Remember that even it if appears to be cloudy or windy the suns rays can penetrate through and cause damage to your skin.

It is important to use a sunblock if you are out and about in the sun. For the first few days use a cream that has total protection and then gradualy reduce this.

If you have been swimming you may need to apply another layer of cream when you leave the pool. During the midday hours you should wear a T-shirt and hat.

Do not forget to protection your eyes. Sunglasses should be worn at all times.

Errors

1   The word **cancer** has been spelt incorrectly.

2   The word **risen** has been spelt incorrectly.

3   The word **passed** has been used instead of **past**.

4   The **s** has been omitted from the word **years**.

5   There are too many spaces after the full stop.

6   There is no space between **of** and **your**.

7   The words **it** and **if** have been transposed.

8   The apostrophe in **sun's** has been omitted.

9   The word **few** has been repeated.

10 The word **gradually** contains a typographical error.

11 The word **swimming** contains a typographical error.

12 The word **protect** has been extended to **protection**.

Proof Reading Exercise 3

CAREERS ADVISORY SERVICE

1 Looking for a new carrer?

> **Come to the**
>
> **CAREER AND EMPLOYMENT FAYRE**
>
> **at The Pavilion**
>
> **6 – 8 March**
>
> **9 am – 8 pm**

2 3 Over 100 exhibitors together with careers advisery expert's will be on hand to give advice in the following career areas.

4 Hospitality and Cattering

5 This covers employment in many different fields.Hotels, restaurants, tourism and
6 travel. We can give advise on the qualifications required and courses available.

7 Administration

8 If you would like to no more about careers in administration we can help. We have a
9 10 number of Modern Apprenticeships places avaialbe in this employment sector.

Computing

11 There are many employment opportunity's in this growth area. Find out how to enter this exciting new market.

Errors

1 The word **career** has been spelt incorrectly.

2 The word **advisory** has been spelt incorrectly.

3 The word **experts** has an unnecessary apostrophe.

4 The word **advise** has been used instead of **advice**.

5 The word **catering** has been spelt incorrectly.

6 There is no space after the full stop.

7 The heading is not consistent with the others – ie it is not underscored.

8 The word **no** has been used instead of **know**.

9 The word **apprenticeships** has been spelt incorrectly.

10 The word **available** has been spelt incorrectly.

11 The word **opportunity's** has been used instead of **opportunities**.

Exam Practice 1 Document 1

Have you ever wished you could build your own home?

YOU CAN!

Many people build their dream homes each year.

HOW DO THEY DO IT?

Come along to the Design and Build™ Show at

The Angel Hotel
LEEDS
Friday, Saturday and Sunday
20 – 22 November
9.00 am – 4.00 pm

Sponsored by Design and Build™ Magazine

Thousands of people build their own home each year. Building your own home may seem to be an unrealistic dream, but it is achievable. How can you do it? Come and talk to the experts and find out.

Booking details can be found on http:/DesignBuild.com.uk

We will be holding workshops on:

- Timber-framed houses
- Finding a suitable building plot
- How to budget for the build
- How to calculate the quantity of materials required.

Advance tickets
Adults – £5.00
Accompanied children under 16 years – Free

Exam Practice 1 Document 2

Building Measurements

The Imperial system of measurement used in Britain for many years evolved over the centuries. Many of these were measured by parts of the body. For example, a yard was the distance from the nose to the end of an outstretched arm. Obviously, this method was not always accurate.

The French introduced the metric system based on more standard measures. Napoleon introduced this system wherever he established his Empire.

Over the years there has been a number of attempts to bring Britain's measuring system into line with other European countries. However, it was not until 1976 that the Weights and Measures Act gave the Government permission to phase out Imperial measurements.

The system gradually being introduced into Britain today is the Système Internationale d'Unités, often abbreviated to SI.

The main advantage of this system is that there is a symbol for each unit. This means that it does not need to be translated into any language.

Although exact conversion figures exist to change Imperial measure into metric, many of these figures include several decimal points. To make conversion easier, figures are often rounded up or down to the nearest whole number or 0.5 ($\frac{1}{2}$).

Exam Practice 1 Document 3 ctd

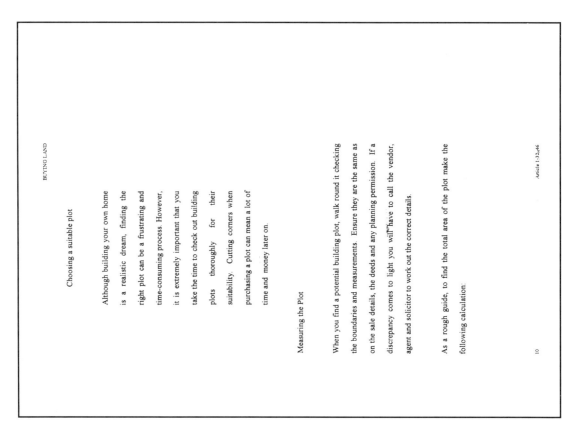

$l \times b = m^2$. If the area is not rectangular, but circular, the calculation is πr^2

breadth

total area

length

This will give you the total plot area. Remember that the proposed dwelling must fit easily onto the plot including access for your vehicles.

Plot Problems

Check the plot for possible problems. These may include ponds, trees, existing foundations, ditches, etc. Assess whether you can deal with these easily or whether they will add thousands of pounds to your building budget. Wet areas or a spring can also cause problems on the plot. However, in dry weather, these may not be obvious immediately. Indicators can be willows, rushes or alders.

Services

If the land already has the main services connected (these are sewerage, gas, water and electricity) check the position of the various manholes, stopcocks and pipes. If these need to be diverted to accommodate your building this could prove expensive.

11

Article 1-32-46

Exam Practice 1 Document 3

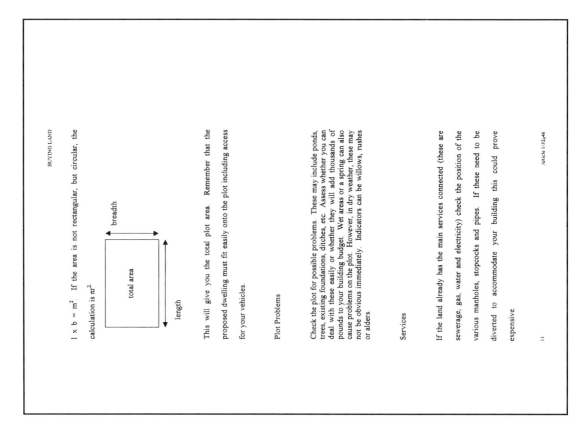

Choosing a suitable plot

Although building your own home is a realistic dream, finding the right plot can be a frustrating and time-consuming process. However, it is extremely important that you take the time to check out building plots thoroughly for their suitability. Cutting corners when purchasing a plot can mean a lot of time and money later on.

Measuring the Plot

When you find a potential building plot, walk round it checking the boundaries and measurements. Ensure they are the same as on the sale details, the deeds and any planning permission. If a discrepancy comes to light you will have to call the vendor, agent and solicitor to work out the correct details.

As a rough guide, to find the total area of the plot make the following calculation:

10

Article 1-32-46

Exam Practice 1 Document 4

Land for Sale

The following plots of land are all suitable for building residential accommodation. For full details including viewing appointments, please contact Louis François, quoting the correct reference number.

COUNTY	PLOT DETAILS	REF NO	PRICE
BERKSHIRE	Grade II listed thatched cottage in need of complete renovation.	BK1	£120,000
	Building plot, ¼ acre with outline planning permission for 2-storey dwelling.	BK2	£110,000
CAMBRIDGESHIRE	Four plots each with a site area of ½ acre. Each has outline planning permission for a detached dwelling.	CM1	£50,000 per plot
	Range of farm buildings on site of approximately ⅓ acre. Detailed planning permission to convert to pair of semi-detached dwellings.	CM2	Offers invited
CHESHIRE	Single building plot with outline planning permission for 3-bedroomed property.	CH1	£39,000
	Building plot in central location measuring approximately 49ft x 117ft. Outline planning permission for detached dwelling.	CH2	£42,000
CORNWALL	Barn with outbuildings on plot of approximately 1 acre. All services are connected and the plot has detailed planning permission for a 4-bedroomed dwelling. Wonderful sea views.	CW1	£130,000
	Plot measuring 100ft x 63ft with lapsed outline planning permission for a single detached dwelling. The plot is located in a village inland.	CW2	£59,000
	Beautiful sea views from this plot measuring 530m². Detailed planning permission for 2-storey, 3-bedroomed dwelling.	CW3	£64,000

Exam Practice 1 Document 3 ctd

BUYING LAND

If there are no existing services check the immediate vicinity to see where they are. Connection fees can be very costly. Bear in mind that you have no automatic right to cross land that does not belong to you in order to connect the services.

Access

Obviously you will need to have satisfactory access to the plot. If you are planning to buy a plot on a private road you will need to obtain access rights. You will also need to have good visibility at the point your drive would join the public highway. As a rough guide take 2½ paces back from this point and check up and down the road. Hedges, telegraph poles, trees and fences may all block your access.

If any of these problems do arise, your solicitor should be able to give you advice on how to solve them.

12

Article 1:32a46

Exam Practice 2 Document 1

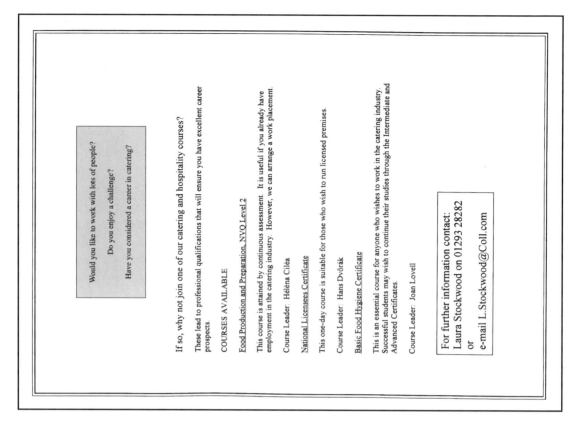

Would you like to work with lots of people?

Do you enjoy a challenge?

Have you considered a career in catering?

If so, why not join one of our catering and hospitality courses?

These lead to professional qualifications that will ensure you have excellent career prospects.

COURSES AVAILABLE

Food Production and Preparation, NVQ Level 2

This course is attained by continuous assessment. It is useful if you already have employment in the catering industry. However, we can arrange a work placement.

Course Leader: Hélèna Cilea

National Licensees Certificate

This one-day course is suitable for those who wish to run licensed premises.

Course Leader: Hans Dvŏrák

Basic Food Hygiene Certificate

This is an essential course for anyone who wishes to work in the catering industry. Successful students may wish to continue their studies through the Intermediate and Advanced Certificates

Course Leader: Joan Lovell

For further information contact:
Laura Stockwood on 01293 28282
or
e-mail L.Stockwood@Coll.com

Exam Practice 1 Document 4 ctd

SUFFOLK

Barn suitable for conversion. Total site area ¼ acre with outline planning permission granted. — SK1 — £85,000

Derelict bungalow requiring demolition. Planning permission unknown. Site measures ⅓ acre. — SK2 — Offers over £65,000

YORKSHIRE

Site for sale totalling 1 acre. Outline planning permission granted for 3 detached, 2-storey dwellings. Owner will split into separate plots. — YK1 — £120,000 or £45,000 per plot

Although we have made every effort to ensure the details given are correct, we strongly recommend you consult a solicitor before entering into a contract.

Lecture Notes[1,2,4]

FOOD HYGIENE

It is essential that all food is handled carefully keeping in mind some basic hygiene rules. This is to prevent bacteria from growing and causing food poisoning.

General Hygiene

In order to ensure basic hygiene in the kitchen you should always follow these basic rules:

- Wash your hands thoroughly before handling food.
- Ensure the work surfaces and utensils are sparkling clean and have been washed in hot, soapy water.
- Use separate chopping boards for raw and cooked foods.

Refrigeration

Most people now own a refrigerator and/or freezer. These are very effective in preventing the growth of bacteria. However, it is important that food is stored correctly and that the appliance is working at the correct temperature.

©George Knight 1998

6

Healthy Eating

This recipe is super for dining al fresco with friends. A warm summer's evening, some good red wine, crusty bread and a mixed green salad is all that is needed to accompany this dish.

Ingredients

4 large aubergines, 300g low-fat mozzarella cheese, 1 jar pesto, 2 tbsps olive oil, ½ litre passata, 2 cloves garlic, 100g cheddar cheese, 1 medium-sized onion, 2 tbsps sun-dried tomato paste, handful chopped basil.

Preparation

Heat the oven to Gas mark 5/190°C/375°F. Slice each aubergine lengthways and brush lightly with the olive oil. Fry until soft. Spread each slice with a little pesto and then place 2 small slices of mozzarella on top. Roll carefully and place into a greased baking dish. Repeat with the rest of the aubergine slices.

Now chop and fry the onion and garlic in a heavy-based saucepan until soft. Add the passata, basil and sun-dried tomato paste and heat through. Pour on top of the aubergine rolls. Sprinkle the grated cheddar cheese on top and bake for 25 – 30 minutes.

Dessert ideas for this meal include lemon and lime cheesecake, summer fruit sorbet or lemon torte.

Bon appetit!

Lecture Notes[2/4]

The position of the food on the shelves should also be taken into consideration. Food should be covered, especially fresh food and liquids. This will help prevent contamination and transference of smells. Place raw foods – especially meat and fish – on the lower shelves. This will stop drips contaminating other foods. It is particularly important that you avoid storing raw and cooked meats together.

Cooking Food

It is important to cook food thoroughly at the correct temperature to ensure bacteria is killed. Food should always be served piping hot.

An oven thermometer can be a good investment as the temperature should be checked regularly to ensure the oven is performing properly. Remember, if you are cooking two or more dishes at the same time, the cooking time may need to be extended.

Cooking times for food – especially raw meat such as poultry – should be calculated accurately. For example, a turkey will need to be cooked for 20 minutes per pound in weight, plus an extra 20 minutes. The calculation you will need to make is:

$(b \times c) + c$ (where $c = 20$ mins $+ b =$ weight in pounds)

©George Knight 1998

8

Lecture Notes[2/4]

Once purchased, chilled or frozen food should be transferred from the shop to your refrigerator as quickly as possible to prevent the food from warming (which allows bacteria to spread).

Once the food is in the refrigerator, it should be stored at the correct temperature. A domestic refrigerator should have a temperature of ≤4°C at all times. This is because food poisoning organisms will grow at temperatures of ≥5°C in a refrigerator or –15°C in a freezer.

If your kitchen is hot, and this applies particularly in warm weather, you may need to adjust the thermostat accordingly. It is worth investing in a suitable thermometer to check that the refrigerator is working correctly.

The position of the refrigerator is also important. If at all possible it should be positioned away from the cooker. It should have a space of at least 50mm from the wall to allow heat to escape.

A good basic kitchen design is as follows:

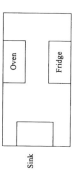

Sink

Oven

Fridge

©George Knight 1998

7

Exam Practice 2 Document 4 ctd

Exam Practice 2 Document 4

Employment Opportunities in Hospitality and Catering

Given below are a few of the jobs we have on offer in the hospitality and catering industry. If you would like to apply for any of these positions, please call Hannah Parslow on 01344 5277612 and quote the appropriate reference number.

HOTELS

HT12 — General Kitchen Assistant required at busy city-centre hotel. Applicant must hold a Basic Food Hygiene Certificate. £4.10 per hour

HT14 — Waiting Staff large country-house hotel requires trained and experienced Silver Service staff. Hours 6.00 pm – midnight, five evenings per week to include Saturdays. Own transport essential. £4.20 per hour

HT22 — Head Chef required to lead team. Small hotel in city-centre location. Salary negotiable

HT25 — Restaurant Manager required for busy hotel restaurant. Applicants should hold a minimum of HND in Hotel, Catering and Industrial Operations. Salary in the range of £18,000 – £20,000.

RESTAURANTS

RT4 — Patissière Chef required at exclusive restaurant situated on outskirts of city. Applicants should hold all relevant qualifications and have had at least three years' experience. Salary negotiable

RT8 — General Kitchen Assistant required for small restaurant in city centre. Four evenings per week, 5.30 pm – 11.30 pm. Transport home provided. £3.75 per hour

RT21 — Vegetarian Chef required for a local vegetarian restaurant. Must be committed to serving delicious meals without meat. £15,000+

RT43 — Waiting Staff required for small, friendly restaurant. No experience required as full training will be given. £3.40 per hour

RT49 — Wine Waiter required for award-winning restaurant, city-centre location. Applicants must hold relevant qualifications. Excellent salary

1

MISCELLANEOUS

M33 — Catering Assistants required for fast-food chain. Experience not necessary as full training will be given. Applicants should be enthusiastic and able to work weekends. In excess of £4.10 per hour

M37 — Catering Assistants required for local hospital. Applicants should have NVQ Level 2 in catering. £3.95 per hour

These are just a few of the positions we have at present. To find out more browse our website at http/jobs@HCI.com.

2

Valley Garden Centre

Summer workshops

We are pleased to announce the latest in a series of workshops These are suitable for both beginners and those with a little experience.

Call Zoë Greening on
01231 928726
for enrolment details

Monday 2 May
10.00 am – 12 noon

Growing Roses

All you need to know about growing roses Whether you wish to grow patio, climber or standard roses When to plant, the varieties available, pruning etc.

Delorés O'Sullivan   £15

Tuesday 3 May
10.00 am – 4.00 pm

Planning a Water Garden

Stephen Andrews will give step-by-step instruction on how to design, build and maintain a water garden. Full details on all necessary equipment will be given.

Stephen Andrews   £45

Tuesday 10 May
10.00 am – 4.00 pm

Planting a Water Garden

This is a follow-on course to Planning a Water Garden. Stephen gives advice on the best plants available for your garden, how and when to plant and the necessary maintenance.

Stephen Andrews   £45

Growing Clematis

There are over 500 different varieties of clematis. How do you choose which plant will be suitable for you? Follow our handy guide given below:

Full Sun

Some plants fade in strong sunlight. To avoid this try Rouge Cardinal or Ernest Markham. Both of these grow to approximately 3m and flower from midsummer to early autumn.

Shade

If you have shady areas in your garden then try Blue Moon. This new variety has large white flowers suffused with pale lilac. It grows to a height of 2½m.

Another variety that is happiest in shade is Blue Belle. This deep violet-purple flowering plant grows to approximately 3¼m. It flowers from July to September.

Ground Cover

To cover patches of ground try this sprawling variety. Pagoda produces creamy pink-mauve flowers from early to late summer and is happy in sun or shade. It is a very hardy plant and grows to a height of 3m.

These are just a few of the clematis that can work well in your garden. There are also varieties that are particularly suitable for growing in containers If you require scented flowers, there are a large number of fragrant plants to choose from. Ask our experienced staff for help and advice.

Exam Practice 3 Document 3

GARDENING FOR BEGINNERS

Soil

Before you start gardening you should find out whether your soil is alkaline or acid. This is governed by the amount of lime contained in the soil. An alkaline soil is rich in lime or chalk, an acid soil lacks lime. The degree of acidity or alkalinity is measured on the pH scale which runs from 0 to 14. The pH is the negative logarithm to base 10 of H^+ ion concentration, calculated using the following formula: $pH = \log_{10}(1/(H^+))$.

A soil with a pH value of 7.0 is called neutral. Values over 7.0 are considered alkaline, lower than 7.0 are acidic. Most plants will grow well with a pH value in the range of 6.0 to 7.0. Simple soil-testing

Exam Practice 3 Document 3 ctd

kits are available that will check the soil's pH value. You should test this regularly.

Climate and Weather

A climate describes a set of conditions prevailing at a given spot over a period. A garden climate depends upon factors such as distance from sea, latitude and winds. A local climate can vary quite widely from the norm of a district. This is called a microclimate.

Plants that will grow in a certain climate are called hardy. This is the resistance to frost and general adaptation to the cycle of seasons in the area. As an example, plants from sub-tropical areas would not be hardy in the UK climate and would need to be protected from cold and frost.

The growing season is defined as the number of days the temperature rises above 6°C (43°F) which is the temperature at which grass begins to grow. Land is divided into zones of growth and Europe varies from zone 2 – which has only 150 growing days per year to zone 10 – where growth is continuous.

Crop Rotation

If the same crop is grown in the same soil from year to year without feeding, then the soil may lack certain essential nutrients and become prone to disease and pests. Rotating the crops grown each year or so

Exam Practice 3 Document 4

Valley Garden Centre

Clematis Promotion

This season we are promoting clematis plants at unbeatable prices. We have a wide variety of plants in stock. Some of our most popular plants are listed below.

Type	Details	Sale Price	Usual Price
SPRING FLOWERING			
Markham's Pink	Deep-pink double flowers, from early to late spring.	£6.99	£10.99
Burford White	Creamy flowers from early to late spring.	£7.99	£8.99
Niobe	Rich deep-red flowers from late spring to early autumn.	£10.99	£12.99
Apple Blossom	Flowers between March and April, wonderful fragrance.	£6.50	£9.99
SUMMER FLOWERING			
Aljonushaka	Rich, mauve-pink flowers from July to September.	£6.99	£8.50
Summer Snow	Flowers between midsummer and mid-autumn. The creamy-white flowers are slightly scented.	£4.75	£5.99
Jackmanni	One of the most popular plants. Deep-purple flowers appear from June to September.	£10.00	£11.50

1

Exam Practice 3 Document 3 ctd

5

GARDENING HINTS AND TIPS

will allow maximum use to be made of the nutrients contained in the soil.

Vegetables are divided into three classes for the purpose of crop rotation. These are shown below:

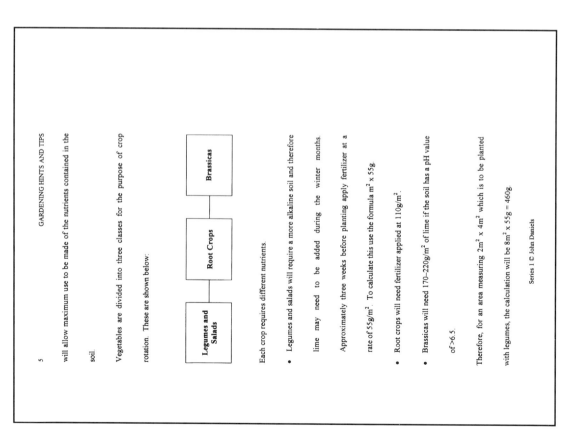

Legumes and Salads — Root Crops — Brassicas

Each crop requires different nutrients.

- Legumes and salads will require a more alkaline soil and therefore lime may need to be added during the winter months.

Approximately three weeks before planting apply fertilizer at a rate of 55g/m^2. To calculate this use the formula m^2 x 55g.

- Root crops will need fertilizer applied at 110g/m^2.

- Brassicas will need 170–220g/m^2 of lime if the soil has a pH value of >6.5.

Therefore, for an area measuring 2m^2 x 4m^2 which is to be planted with legumes, the calculation will be 8m^2 x 55g = 460g.

Series 1 © John Daniels

Exam Practice 3 Document 4 ctd

Ourika Valley   £5.99   £8.25

This is a hardy plant that has pale-yellow flowers.

Freckles   £7.75   £9.00

As its name suggests, this has heavily-speckled, creamy-pink flowers. Much prettier than the description.

You will find many more varieties in our nursery. However, if you would like a particular species then we can order it for you. Please ask at our Customer Services desk.

3

Exam Practice 3 Document 4 ctd

Ascotiensus   £5.50   £7.99

Bright-blue flowers throughout summer.

Polish Spirit   £6.50   £9.25

This clematis is suitable for container planting and flowers from midsummer to autumn. Its flowers are rich purple-blue.

AUTUMN FLOWERING

Etoile Violette   £4.00   £4.85

Large flowers which are violet-purple with a reddish tint.

Petit Faucon   £10.50   £12.50

This is excellent value as it flowers for over three months. The flowers are a beautiful deep blue with yellow-orange stamens when young.

Wyevale   £4.25   £7.00

This has dark-blue, scented flowers that last from August to October.

WINTER FLOWERING

Wisley Cream   £3.50   £5.00

This has light-green leaves with greenish-cream flowers.

Cirrhosa balearica   £7.50   £9.00

The green foliage of this plant turns to bronze during winter. As an added bonus, its creamy pink flowers are fragrant.

2

Exam Practice 4 Document 1

CRAFT NEWS

Craft News is a specialist magazine featuring all types of craft work.

The magazine is packed with features including:

step-by-step guides
patterns and scale drawings for craft projects
hints and tips by experts
where to buy
what to look for:

> Monthly
> Price £2.95

The September issue of Craft News has the first of a 7-part series on ceramics. This special supplement tells you all you need to know to start this fascinating hobby or to improve your existing skills.

The series will look at the history, materials, equipment, tools, glazing, firing and decoration techniques. Some of the best-known experts in this subject will be revealing the secrets of their success.

A chance to win a weekend course at one of the country's leading studios is also on offer.

Next issue on sale 7 September.

Exam Practice 4 Document 2

Porcelain

We can all enjoy the beauty of a well-sculpted and painted piece of porcelain. It first appeared in China in the 7th century during the reign of the T'ang dynasty.

Porcelain came to Europe via Palestine during the Crusades and was literally worth its weight in gold. Many people believed it had magical powers. A common superstition was that if a poisoned drink were poured into porcelain it would shatter the drinking vessel.

Early, detailed reports of porcelain manufacture were brought to Europe in 1295, and attempts were made to copy it.

However it took until the end of the 17th century before soft frit porcelain was made in France. The formula for hard porcelain was discovered in 1709

by Johann Friedrich Böttger in Meissen.

By the end of the 18th century, frit porcelain was manufactured under the name of pâte tendre artificielle, at Sèvres, France. The formula had been invented in 1673 and manufactured in 1695 by Pierre Chicaneau in his Saint-Cloud factory.

Bone china, which was invented by an Englishman, Thomas Frye, in 1748 will be the subject of the second article in this fascinating series.

Exam Practice 4 Document 3

Guide to Ceramics Part I

The basic materials used for the manufacture of ceramics are clay and kaolin.

According to composition, use, firing, temperature and deformation in fire, they can be classified as various types of clay. These are:

- brick
- earthenware
- porous (whiteware)
- stoneware
- porcelain.

These clays are often used as components of man-made ceramic bodies.
Ceramic working bodies can be either plastic or non-plastic.

Plastic Materials

These are fine-ground rocks formed by clay materials whose particles are less than 2mm in size. The basic property of these materials is their ability, when mixed with water, to form a mouldable body. It does not develop cracks when bent, and retains its shape when dried and fired.

However, a ceramic body composed only of plastic materials would also have its drawbacks. These include shrinkage and poor drying. In order to overcome these problems, Grog and fluxes are added to the basic composition.

Kaolin

Kaolin is a soft, white, earthy material that is dry to the touch. When mixed with water it becomes fairly plastic and retains its colour when fired. Kaolin is

---

Exam Practice 4 Document 3 ctd

refractory (fire-resistant). It is usually produced by kaolinization (weathering) of feldspathic rocks. Its basic component is the rock kaolinite $A_2_2O_3.2SiO_2.2H_2O$.

Primary Clays

These are a mixture of clay minerals according to the exact composition of the parent rock and its means of decomposition.

Secondary Clays

These are clays that have been transported from the original site of formation.
The main agent of transportation is water.

Fireclays

These withstand very high temperatures of at least 1580°C. Fireclays are normally used for furnace lining and other technical purposes.

Other secondary clays include stoneware, earthenware, brick, Marls and Bentonitic.

Ceramic Batches

Most clays need to be processed before use. Once prepared the ceramic batch should be easy to shape, have low shrinkage and keep its shape when fired. More information on processing will be given later in the series.

Exam Practice 4 Document 4

CLASSIFIED ADVERTISEMENTS

The advertisements listed below have been booked for the September Ceramic Supplement. The copy and rough drafts have already been sent to the designer.

COPY	CONTACT NAME	SIZE	PRICE	TYPE
EXETER CERAMICS We can supply all types of clay, glazes, tools and equipment. Competitive prices and free delivery within the Exeter area.	Duncan MacDonald	¼ page	£450	Ceramic Suppliers
JOHN AND JOAN HANSFORD For all your ceramic needs. We stock the largest range of materials at the lowest prices. Delivery guaranteed within 4 days of order.	Joan Hansford	$\frac{1}{3}$ page	£675	Ceramic Suppliers
VINTON LTD Suppliers of raw materials for all types of glazes. Trade enquiries only. For full details call 01721 564632.	Lorraine Swift	$\frac{1}{8}$ page	£250	Glaze Specialists
CARLTON POTTERY If you are interested in learning more about this fascinating craft, then try one of our courses. We offer day, evening, weekend and residential courses. Suitable for beginners and improvers. For further information on our wide range of courses, call 0138 2839183.	Peter Richards	Full page	£1500	Specialist Courses
GEORGE LEWIS STUDIO For courses on decoration techniques visit my studio in Taunton. Our specially-designed workshops are suitable for beginners to advanced students. All materials are included in workshop fees. One-day courses start at £85. Contact George Lewis on 01239 4242771 for details of our winter courses.	George Lewis	Full page	£2000	Specialist Courses

1

Exam Practice 4 Document 3 ctd

Craft News Supplement

Testing

Testing your ceramic materials before use is essential. This will also be featured fully later on in the series. However, as an example, we will look at the shrinkage test.

First of all make a bar from the ceramic material and mark a precise line, 10cm will be sufficient. See Fig. 1.

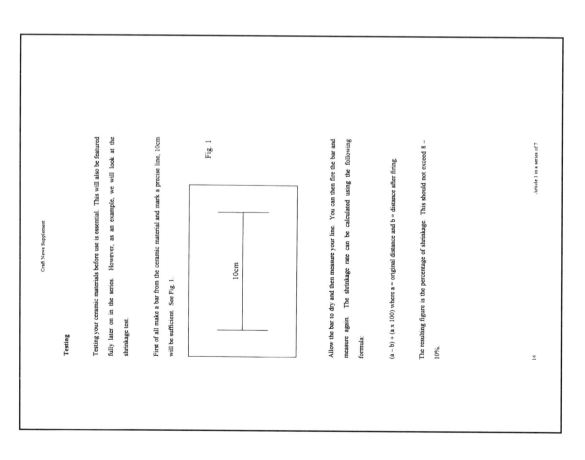

Fig. 1

Allow the bar to dry and then measure your line. You can then fire the bar and measure again. The shrinkage rate can be calculated using the following formula:

$(a – b) \div (a \times 100)$ where a = original distance and b = distance after firing.

The resulting figure is the percentage of shrinkage. This should not exceed 8 – 10%.

14

Exam Practice 5 Document 1

H₂O Cruises™

In association with

The Preferred Travel Company
Bath Branch

Invite you to a cruise evening

on

21 May

at

The Preferred Travel Company, High Street, Bath

8.00 pm	Video presentation – see some of the fabulous cruises for yourself. The video shows each of the company's major ships.
8.30 pm	Refreshments
9.00 pm	An opportunity to ask questions and book the cruise of a lifetime.

This is an exciting opportunity to find out more about the wonderful H₂O Cruises™ holidays. Mr David Krüger, Managing Director, will be on hand to answer any of your questions.

Special deals available for customers who book a holiday at the event.

Win a luxury cruise
Free draw for a 7-night Italian Cruise

Exam Practice 4 Document 4 ctd

CHILDREN'S POTTERY Our pottery workshops are very popular with children aged 8 to 14. Classes are limited to 5 children and cost £45 for a 3-hour session. All materials are provided although children will need to bring protective clothing. Courses held each day during the school holidays. To book a place telephone 01813 2837162. (Bath area).	Margaret Seymour	¼ page	£450	General Courses
THE POTTER'S WHEEL ™ Suppliers of quality equipment to trade and general public. Personal callers to our warehouse are welcome. Opening hours 10 am – 5 pm, Monday to Saturday. Alternatively, browse through our fully-illustrated catalogue and price list. Our prices are always competitive. The Potter's Wheel™ Studio, Brick Lane, Lowestoft. Telephone Mick Bennett on 01282 242628 for further information.	Mick Bennett	½ page	£900	Ceramic Suppliers

2

Report on Trading – H₂O Cruises™

The H₂O Cruises™ division of the corporation has had an excellent trading year. The increase in passenger numbers exceeded target and the majority of cruises were booked to capacity. The increased number of bookings meant that turnover has gone up by 35%. Enquiries for cruise holidays also increased dramatically. This has been estimated to be over 45%.

Over 10,000 customers received a questionnaire after they had completed their holiday. The response rate was high with 52% of customers responding. From these replies we have been able to analyse our customers' needs and it is hoped that we will be able to act upon their suggestions in the coming year.

Some of the more important points are given below.

Many customers felt that the service given by our crew was excellent. However, 1/3 felt that improvements could be made with regard to the slow service at meal times.

Cleanliness of some areas of the ship(s) was also an issue, in particular

on the Fiesta. Of the 1600 replies from Fiesta clients, over 1/4 felt that the decks and walkways were not cleaned to a satisfactory standard. This has been investigated and it is anticipated that this issue has been resolved.

The current market share held by H₂O Cruises™ has been calculated to be 29%. This was calculated using the following formula. Obviously all figures are estimates.

η = tm (total market) ÷ np (number of passengers on H₂O Cruises™)

---

7   Information Sheet

CRUISING HOLIDAYS

Taking a cruise may seem to many of us to be beyond our budget.

However, this is not the case. A cruise can be as affordable as any

package holiday.

British holidaymakers are beginning to appreciate the fun that can be

had on a cruise. Approximately 650,000 British people took a cruise

holiday in 1997 compared with 298,000 in 1993. However, as around

17 million British people booked a package holiday in 1997, it can be

seen that cruises have room to improve their market share.

Cost

The price of a 7-night cruise can cost as little as £500 per person.

When you take into account that all meals, entertainment and

children's facilities are included in this price, this can compare

favourably with other types of holiday.

Ref I²346A

---

9   Information Sheet

Destinations

You can take a cruise to almost anywhere. Many tour operators offer a two-part holiday. This gives you the opportunity to spend half your holiday at sea and the rest at a hotel.

The length of the cruise varies enormously from a three-night break to a worldwide cruise lasting several months.

Popular destinations include Jamaica, Barbados, the Greek Islands and even Florida.

Accommodation

There is a wide choice of accommodation on board most ships. This generally ranges from a small cabin with private bathroom to large suites, which include a sitting room, bedroom and bathroom. Outside cabins – those which are facing the sea – cost more than inside cabins.

It is possible to book a 4-berth cabin, these are great for families with young children.

Ref $1^2$346A

8   Information Sheet

Entertainment

These days most cruises offer plenty of opportunity to visit new places by having a well-planned itinerary. For the few days you are confined on board the ship there are plenty of activities on offer.

You can take your pick from gymnasiums, theatres, cinemas, deck sports, lectures and swimming.

As some of the larger ships have over 2,000 passengers it is unlikely you will become bored. There will always be someone who is willing to have a drink or exchange stories with you.

Activity Cruises

If you enjoy an active holiday or like to learn new skills, then why not combine these with a cruise? There are many different cruises available which combine both. The activities on offer include creative writing, painting, health and beauty – something to suit all tastes.

Ref $1^2$346A

Exam Practice 5 Document 4

H²O Cruises™

June Vacations

Given below are just a few of the cruises we offer. These vacations all have a start date in June. For further information contact Elizabeth Chaine on 01727 4422176.

SHIP	DETAILS	PRICE PER PERSON FROM	NUMER OF NIGHTS
ST LUCIA	Fly to Orlando and meet your ship at Fort Lauderdale. The ship docks at Nassau, San Juan, St John and St Thomas, Half Moon Cay returning to Fort Lauderdale. Return flight from Orlando.	£750	7
FIESTA	This cruise offers a variety of towns, islands and beaches to ensure you enjoy the best of the Carribean. You can enjoy shopping in some of the great cities followed by exploring unspoilt islands.	£1675	14
	Fly to Montego Bay to meet the Fiesta for an action-packed voyage. Ports of call include Santa Domingo, British Virgin Island Tortola, Antigua, Dominica, St Lucia, Grenada, Barbados, St Vincent, Guadeloupe, St Kitts, Serena Cay. The Fiesta then returns to Montego Bay for your flight back to the UK.		15
PRESIDENT	Our Italian cruise is excellent value for money. It is a 7-night cruise but can be extended with a 7-night stay on land.	£720 or	7 or 14
	Fly to Palma to join the President. The ship calls at Rome, Naples, Messina (Sicily), Malta and Sardinia. You then return to Palma for your flight home or to transfer to your chosen accommodation.	£1300	

1

Exam Practice 5 Document 3 ctd

10   Information Sheet

Given below is a typical cabin layout.

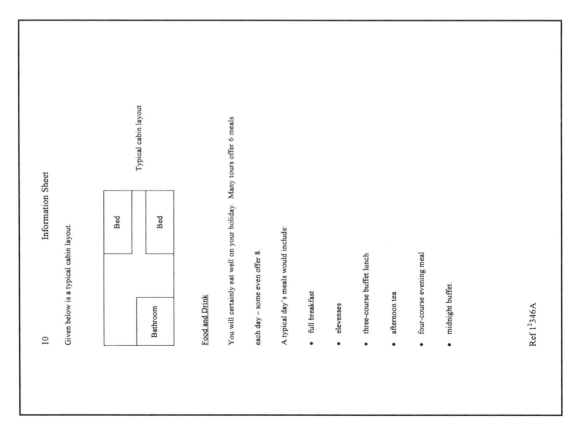

Typical cabin layout

Food and Drink

You will certainly eat well on your holiday. Many tours offer 6 meals each day – some even offer 8.

A typical day's meals would include:

- full breakfast
- elevenses
- three-course buffet lunch
- afternoon tea
- four-course evening meal
- midnight buffet.

Ref 1²346A

Exam Practice 6 Document 1

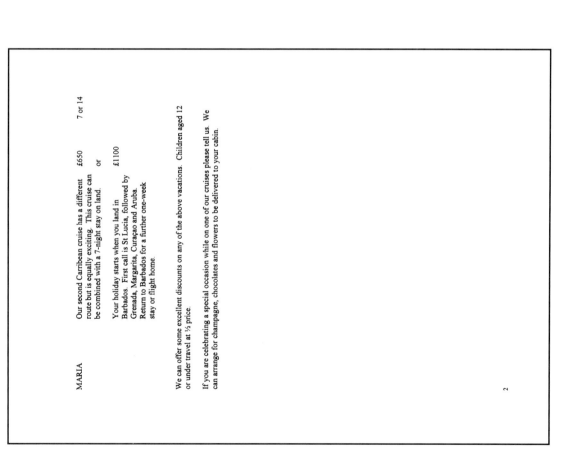

LIFE STYLE MAGAZINE

The third edition of our quarterly magazine

SUMMER SPECIAL
HEALTH AND BEAUTY ISSUE

All you need to know – the latest ideas and articles on

Keeping Fit   Sports, equipment, exercise. The latest in sports crazes.
Where to find the equipment, where to go.

Looking Good   The latest in fashion, make-up, hair and style.

Feeling Great   Healthy recipes, together with the latest health up-dates.

Features on:

hay fever
stress
healthy eating
the most fashionable places to holiday
the latest activity holidays

Price £2.75

Order a copy from your newsagent now!

Everything you need to keep you looking good and feeling great throughout the summer.

Make-up advice for a natural-looking summer from the professional make-up artists.

Having a bad hair day? We test the most fashionable hair salons.

Exam Practice 5 Document 4

MARIA   Our second Carribean cruise has a different   £650   7 or 14
route but is equally exciting. This cruise can
be combined with a 7-night stay on land.   or

Your holiday starts when you land in   £1100
Barbados. First call is St Lucia, followed by
Grenada, Margarita, Curaçao and Aruba.
Return to Barbados for a further one-week
stay or flight home.

We can offer some excellent discounts on any of the above vacations. Children aged 12 or under travel at ½ price.

If you are celebrating a special occasion while on one of our cruises please tell us. We can arrange for champagne, chocolates and flowers to be delivered to your cabin.

2

Exam Practice 6 Document 3

Healthy Eating

In the past the most usual way to calculate if you were overweight was to use a weight table. However, this is not the most accurate method, as it does not take into account various other factors such as your build.

The recommended way to calculate your body weight is the Body Mass Index (BMI). It is calculated by dividing the weight in kilograms by the square of the height in metres.

To do this, weigh yourself in kilograms and measure your height in metres. Divide your weight by your height in m^2. For example, for a person who weighs 65kg and has a height of 1.6m the calculation would be:

$65 \div 1.6^2 (1.6 \times 1.6) = 65 \div 2.56 = 25.4$

The final figure is your BMI and you compare it to the following:

- BMI 20 or below – Underweight
- BMI 20 – 24.9 – Normal
- BMI 25 – 29.9 – Plump
- BMI 30 – 39.9 – Moderately overweight
- BMI 40 and above – Very overweight

Special Issue

Exam Practice 6 Document 2

Hay Fever

If you are one of Britain's 3 million hay fever sufferers, you will appreciate how this can ruin your summer, making you a virtual prisoner indoors. The number of sufferers of this summer complaint has doubled over the past 10 years.

What is it?

Hay fever is an allergic response to pollen. This can be from trees, grasses and flowers. The allergic reaction occurs when the immune system treats the pollen particles as allergens – invaders.

What are the symptoms?

Common symptoms include:

- itchy or weeping eyes
- rhinitis (inflammation of the nasal passages)
- sneezing.

These are caused by the body responding to the allergens.

Can it be treated?

The good news is that hay fever can be treated successfully. There are a number of treatments on the market that you can buy over the counter at your local pharmacist. However, if your symptoms persist it is always worth visiting your GP.

Conventional Medicine

The most common treatment is by antihistamines, which will help reduce weeping eyes and nose. However, you may need a decongestant as well. Although antihistamine is a powerful remedy, many of the medicines can also cause side effects. These may include drowsiness and insomnia.

Alternative Treatment

There are many alternative treatments that claim to alleviate the symptoms of hay fever. Some of the most common are homeopathy and acupuncture.

Exam Practice 6 Document 3 ctd

If your calculation tells you that you have a BMI of 25 or over then you may wish to lose some weight. It is very important that you consult your GP before entering into any type of diet.

If you do decide to lose some weight then adopt a sensible eating plan. You should include plenty of fresh vegetables and salads, together with protein and fibre-giving foods such as meat, bread, fish, cheese, etc. Try to cut down on the sugar- or fat-loaded foods such as sweets, chocolate, crisps, fizzy drinks and alcohol. Your GP will be able to advise you on a sensible, healthy eating plan.

Vitamins and Minerals

It is important that you have a diet rich in vitamins and minerals. These help your body stay fit and healthy. Green vegetables are a good source of vitamins B_2 and C.

Cereals are also a good source of the B vitamins such as B_{12} and B_6. They also contain minerals such as iron and folic acid. For example, a 30 g serving of cereal with 125 ml of semi-skimmed milk can provide 75μ of iron, that is 75% of the recommended daily allowance (RDI).

Carbohydrates

The main carbohydrates are glucose ($C_6H_{12}O_6$), fructose (found in fruit), starch, sugar and cellulose (found in plants).

Exam Practice 6 Document 3 ctd

These are essential energy-giving foods. Although most carbohydrates are good for us, foods high in sugar should be eaten in moderation.

Fats

These are also energy-giving foods but, because of their high cholesterol and calorie values, should be eaten in moderation. These foods include butter, margarine, cooking oil, some processed foods such as crisps and foods that have been fried.

Proteins

Milk, eggs, cheese, fish, pulses and nuts all contain proteins. These are body-building foods that assist growth and repair damaged tissue. Muscles, skin, hair and nails are all nearly 100% protein.

Exam Practice 6 Document 3 ctd

LIFESTYLE   25

To maintain a healthy diet it is recommended that you eat the following portions daily.

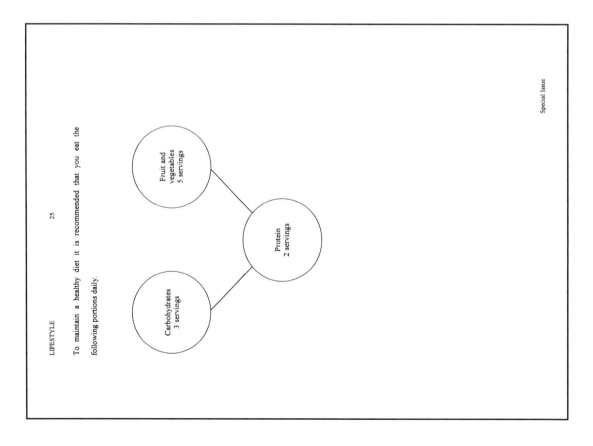

- Carbohydrates 3 servings
- Fruit and vegetables 5 servings
- Protein 2 servings

Special Issue

Exam Practice 6 Document 4

The Most Fashionable Salons

Our intrepid reporter Françoise Page was sent to investigate some of the most fashionable salons.

As she feels her hair is already perfect she asked four testers to have various treatments. Here are the results. The star rating is 5 = excellent, 1 = poor.

		Star Rating
EUGÈNE London	The tester, Louise decided to have a complete restyle of her shoulder-length hair. Clutching a photo of an unsuitable style she ventured in.	****
	Eugène's senior stylist had a 15-minute consultation with Louise. She gently but firmly told Louise that her suggested style would not suit her and gave several alternatives. Louise was thrilled with her new hair style and the service she received.	
JOHN AND JANE Manchester	Kathy was our tester in Manchester. She decided to have a restyle and blonde highlights put through her rather mousy-coloured hair. Kathy mentioned this when booking the appointment and was asked to have a consultation prior to the appointment being booked.	*****
	The stylist and colourist both talked through the various options and a style, colour and appointment were agreed upon. Result? Kathy looks fabulous and feels it was well worth the expense.	
GREENS York	Roberta booked an appointment for her long hair to be styled for a special night out. She explained to the stylist how she wanted her hair to look and sat back to relax. One hour later she emerged feeling happy with the result but extremely unhappy with the price of £55.	**

1

Exam Practice 7 Document 1

Are you fed up with working for someone else?

Would you like to be your own boss?

Find out more at the

BUSINESSPLUS® EXHIBITION

This year's Businessplus® Exhibition offers you the opportunity to find out how to become your own boss and run a successful business.

Franchising is the modern way to start a business as many of the usual risks have been eliminated.

Your initial investment may be as little as £5,000.

We will be offering the following workshops for those interested in franchising.

Saturday 11.00 am   Service Industry

There are a number of service industry opportunities. These range from estate management to financial advice. Investment can be as little as £8,500.

Sunday 2.00 am   Commercial Cleaning

This is a major growth area in franchising. Start-up costs can be as little as £2,000.

For further details on the Exhibition, contact Sîan Davies on 01827 3388119.

Exam Practice 6 Document 4 ctd

*

HEAD MASTERS
Bristol

Suzy tested this fairly new salon. Suzy already has a perm and colour on her hair but decided to try highlights as well. She booked an appointment with David, a senior stylist.

David did not comment upon the condition of Suzy's hair or ask questions about her previous treatments. The result is that her hair is now dry and split and the highlights cannot be seen.

When Suzy complained, she was treated in an off-hand manner and the manager would not reduce the fee of £65.

2

Exam Practice 7 Document 3

Business Information Sheet, 68299

BUSINESS FRANCHISING

What is Franchising?

Franchising in its most basic form is an arrangement between one party, who has a blueprint and system for a business, and a second party who wishes to copy the business.

The franchisor – the person or company with the idea and system – should have developed a tested blueprint for a successful business. They will have investigated the market, developed the product or service and attained the skills necessary to make the business a success.

The franchisee – the person who wishes to copy the business – should receive training to run their business and be offered help and advice from the franchisor when necessary.

Author R. Mañoso

Exam Practice 7 Document 2

Franchising

All franchises work in the same way – that is, the franchisee pays to use the business services, goods and name provided by the franchisor. However, there are a number of different types of franchise.

These include:

Investment

These require a substantial amount of capital to be invested by the franchisee. Usually the franchisee will employ staff, including managerial, to run the business on a day-to-day basis. Often large food or hotel chains are run in this way.

Executive

These are generally the white-collar business services, including financial services, consultancy and personnel. These are often managed by just one person. However, it is best to have had previous experience in the chosen field.

Retail

Retail franchises often require a high level of capital investment. This is because premises, shop fittings and stock all need to be purchased. The benefit of a retail franchise is that the business can usually be sold as a going concern should the owner wish to retire or capitalise on his or her investment. The franchisee generally takes an active role in the business.

There are also other types of franchise such as sales and distribution that can be set up with relatively little capital.

Exam Practice 7 Document 3 ctd

What are the Benefits of Franchising?

As previously mentioned, the franchisee should be given full training in the business and be able to ask for help when needed.

This means it is an ideal way to start running your own business as you should be supported by a group of people who have already assessed the market.

Some franchisors offer their franchisees an exclusive territory so that competition is limited. It is of course in the franchisor's interests to have successful franchisees.

What do I Need to Start my own Business?

In order to make a success of your business you will need the following:

- Capital. As well as your initial investment you will also need money to live on while you are setting up your business.

- Time and effort. Running your own business takes a great deal of time and effort, especially when you first start. If you wish to work nine to five, five days a week, then maybe you are not suited to running a business.

3

Exam Practice 7 Document 3 ctd

- Experience. Many franchisees have not had previous experience in running a business in their market area. However, in order to maximise your chances of success you should try to find a business that capitalises on your existing skills.

What are the Drawbacks of Franchising?

You must put in a great deal of time and commitment on building up your business. This means long hours, often unsociable. This can often put a strain on family life, so you will need support and often practical help from your friends and family.

As the franchisor may take a percentage of your turnover, you will need to generate a larger turnover in order to provide an income sufficient for your needs.

For example, if the franchise agreement states that you must pay, say 3% of your turnover in fees, you will need to increase turnover by approximately 5% in order to achieve the same level of success as a non-franchised business.

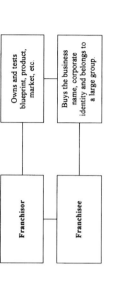

4

Exam Practice 7 Document 4 ctd

		Action
4.2 Visitors	This will be delayed until the required no. of bookings have been made.	
	(Paul Douglas arrived at 3.20 pm)	
5 Printing	The printing of information packs for traders can now be confirmed. It is anticipated that approximately 1000 will be required. After some discussion, it was agreed the contract for printing should be given to Marshall & Co. LB to make the final arrangements.	LB
6 Security	The exhibition centre confirmed that they can provide all necessary security personnel if required. This is at a cost of £1600 per day. DR to consider alternative arrangements.	DR
7 Any Other Business	There were no other matters arising.	
8 Date of Next Meeting	This will be held on 21 December in the exhibition room at 3.00 pm.	
	The meeting closed at 5.00 pm.	

Exam Practice 7 Document 4

Minutes of Meeting of the Exhibition Committee

Held on 21 October
at 3.00 pm
at Businessplan® Head Office

Present: Carrie Lyon, Laurence Brady, Hamish Grant, Deborah Raul

Apologies: Michael Read, Paul Douglas (late arrival)

		Action
1 Minutes of Last Meeting	These were agreed and signed.	
2 Matters Arising	Booking of exhibition centre. DR confirmed that the exhibition centre has accepted our booking and that all services requested can be provided.	
3 Costings	CL reported that, having received confirmation of costs from the exhibition centre, it is now possible to calculate the charges to both exhibitors and visitors. This is calculated as follows:	CL
	$c \div o \div e = \eta$	
	(exhibition centre charges + other overheads ÷ number of exhibitors = break-even point)	
	From this it should be possible to ensure a profit of approximately 25% after the visitors' entrance fees have been added. CL to give a detailed breakdown to all concerned as soon as possible.	
4 Advertising		
4.1 Trade Stands	This was discussed at some length. Invitations to book stands will be sent to all regular exhibitors. New franchisees will also be invited. These must go out within the next few weeks in order to maximise bookings. Overseas companies should be contacted before the end of the month.	CL
	Once CL has calculated the break-even point the intensity of the advertising can be discussed.	

Exam Practice 8 Document 1

AGENDA AND NOTES FOR CHAIR

> Home Features Team Meeting
> to be held on 18 August
> at 2.30 pm in the Conference Room

1   Apologies

2   Minutes of Previous Meeting

3   Matters Arising

    Check that Lorraine Hughes has confirmed the booking of a house at St Ives
    for the Christmas by the Sea feature.

4   November Issue Car Boot Bargains

    Simon Kevill to report on progress. Check that Simon has contacted a
    celebrity interior designer and a stylist for the photographic shoot next month.

5   Planning – Jan to March Issues

    Feature reports to be given by Simon, Lorraine and Melanie. The list of
    proposed features will be circulated within the next few days. Advance
    material to be prepared within three weeks.

6   Any Other Business

7   Date of Next Meeting

    Suggest 22 of next month at 10.00 am in the Conference Room.

Exam Practice 8 Document 2

INTERIOR DECORATION

If you wish to brighten up your home but do not have too much money to spend, why
not try a paint technique on your walls. Paint techniques such as colourwashing,
stencilling, stippling and sponging are all relatively easy to do and cost little. You
will however, need a steady hand, time and patience.

Before you start, make sure that you
prepare your walls properly. If you are
not going to remove any existing
wallpaper, you will have to wash the
walls thoroughly. Use a solution of
sugar soap and water. This is to
remove any greasy marks that may
affect the paint adhering to the paper.

Should you decide to remove the
existing wallpaper, ensure you remove
all traces, especially around light
switches and skirting boards. You may
need to remove or repair any missing
or loose patches of plaster.

There are a number of good DIY books specialising in paint techniques on the market,
or you can ask at your local DIY store for advice. Follow any instructions carefully
and always allow paint to dry thoroughly before applying a second or subsequent
coat.

You can experiment with the various paint techniques until you find one that is right
for your home.

Exam Practice 8 Document 3

Interior Design - Materials   11

HOME DECORATION

Calculating the Materials Required

If you are planning to decorate a room you will need to work out the amount of materials required.

It is important that you purchase the correct amount before you start work as the shades of paint may vary slightly from batch to batch. Different types of paint such as emulsion or gloss will cover different areas depending on its consistency. Your local DIY store will be able to give advice on this.

Paint

As a general rule a standard can will contain one litre of paint.

To decide how much paint to buy, calculate the area to be

©Laura Morris January 1998

Exam Practice 8 Document 3 ctd

Interior Design - Materials   12

painted by multiplying the height by the width of each wall and then add all the totals together.

For example, for a room with two walls measuring 9 ft high x 12 ft wide and two walls measuring 9 ft high x 10 ft wide, the calculation will be (9 x 12) x 2 + (9 x 10) x 2. This will give an answer of 396 ft^2.

To calculate the paint needed for moulded window or door frames, multiply the height by the width of the frames and consider it as a solid surface. For example, for a window measuring 4 ft high x 3 ft wide, the calculation will be 4 x 3 = 12 ft^2.

To paint a moulded door, multiply the height of the door by the width and add one quarter to allow for the increased surface area caused by the moulding. (h x w = a (a ÷ 4 = b) + b = c). For

©Laura Morris January 1998

Exam Practice 8 Document 3 ctd

example, for a door measuring 6 ft high x 3 ft wide, the

calculation will be 6 x 3 = 18 ft², divided by 4 = 4 ½ ft². Now

add the original total of 18 ft² to ¼ to ¼ (4 ½ ft) and the answer will

be 22 ½ ft².

Moulded Door

Types of Paint

There are many different types of paint available, and most have a specific use, for example, paints for wood, walls, pipes and guttering. You will need to find out the type of paint most suitable for the surface you are covering.

The amount of paint you buy will depend on many factors. For

example, you will need to buy more paint if any of the following

apply:

- the type of paint being used is particularly porous

- the area being covered is textured

Exam Practice 8 Document 3 ctd

Once you have calculated the room measurements you should be

able to obtain advice from your local DIY store on how much

paint will be required, bearing in mind the factors given above.

As well as these factors, keep in mind that different types of

paint will cover different amounts of surface area. For example,

a one litre can of emulsion or non-drip gloss paint will cover an

area of 12 m² or 130 ft².

Café Expresso	For a fashionable, stylish look try lots of stainless steel. Many large kitchen appliances are now available with a steel finish, or you can achieve the effect with smaller electrical appliances such as toasters and kettles. This look needs a minimalist approach, so if you like lots of clutter then it may not be right for you. The Lotus chain has the best range of steel accessories on the market.	Lotus 0139 493987

2

COLOUR SCHEMES

It can be difficult choosing a colour scheme that is right for your home. The following list gives some suggestions together with our favourite ranges available at the moment.

BEDROOM		CONTACT
Cool Blue	Try a cool blue bedroom using cornflower blue paint for walls with a crisp white for doors, skirtings and ceilings. The Country Flowers range by Hilton-Smith Designs contains a variety of bedlinen, wallpapers and curtains that would complement this colour scheme.	Hilton-Smith 0121 2882919
Arabian Nights	For a dramatic and striking bedroom use strong colours and luxurious fabrics. Silks and satins will bring instant glamour to your bedroom. Try the Midnight Magic range from Charlotte Evans for brilliant jewel-colour bedspreads, cushions and fabrics.	Charlotte Evans 0382 192893

LIVING ROOM

Classic Lines	Use any of the neutral colours and shades such as beige, cream or ivory for a cool, classic feel. Complement with neutral cushions and curtains made from natural fibres such as linen or raw silk. The Elegant range from Stylish Homes contains a wide range of curtains and cushions in linen, cotton and muslin.	Available from all branches of Russells 0583 563207
Mellow Yellow	Pale lemon gives a warm and light feel to any room. In fact using lemon paint can make a room seem lighter than white. It is a good contrast to many other colours. The best range of lemon and yellow paints can be found at Pierre Pelletier	Pierre Pelletier 0932 451309

KITCHEN

Country Cottage	If you like the idea of a country cottage you can easily recreate this in your home by the use of accessories. Bunches of dried herbs and copper saucepans will help you achieve the look. The Farmhouse range of kitchen accessories is excellent.	Available at most branches of Sébastien Haramée 01827 634501

1